Christmas Cooking for Kids

Anusha A

Author's Note

Dear Readers

THERE IS LOT TO EXPERIENCE IN LIFETIME – START EXPLORE!!

As you embark on your path to success, keep in mind that you have the ability to attain your goals and desires. You will have challenges and setbacks along the way, but it is critical that you remain resilient and keep going forward. Each difficulty provides an opportunity for growth and learning, and each step puts you closer to your objectives. Be confident in yourself and your ability. You are capable of great things, and your distinct abilities and characteristics have the ability to positively impact the world around you. Accept your full potential and dare to dream large. Find inspiration in the stories of people who overcame adversity and succeeded despite the odds. Their stories serve as reminders that with determination, perseverance, and hard work, anything is possible. Surround yourself with happiness and encouragement. Seek for mentors, friends, and colleagues who can encourage and motivate you on your journey. Their advice, wisdom, and support can give you the inspiration you need to keep going, even when things get rough. Remember to acknowledge your progress and accomplishments along the way, no matter how minor they may appear. Each achievement is a credit to your hard work and commitment. Above all, trust in the journey and have faith in yourself. Believe that you are deserving of success and that your efforts will be rewarded in due time. Keep striving, keep believing, and never lose sight of the vision you have for your life. You are capable, you are resilient, and you are destined for greatness. Let your journey be guided by courage, optimism, and a relentless pursuit of your dreams. The world is waiting for you to shine your light brightly and make your mark. Keep going, keep growing, and never lose sight of the incredible potential that lies within you.

With warmest wishes for your success.

[Ms. Anusha]

Introduction

A high-protein diet can be a game changer for anyone looking to enhance their health, develop muscle, or lose weight. Protein is a key building block of the body, helping in muscle repair, growth, and overall bodily function.

A high-protein diet can help you achieve your goals, whether you're an athlete hoping to improve your performance, a person looking to lose weight, or simply want to maintain a healthy diet.

It might be difficult for beginners to find out how to incorporate additional protein into their regular diet. This guide is intended to make things easier by presenting delicious, simple, and nutritious high-protein meals to fit a variety of tastes and diets.

From hearty breakfasts to simple lunches and fulfilling dinners, these recipes guarantee you get enough protein while eating flavorful, well-balanced meals.

High-protein diets do not need to be complicated or restricted. With a little ingenuity and the correct ingredients, you can make meals that are not only high in protein but also delicious and full.

This collection of recipes is ideal for novices, with step-by-step directions that make cooking simple and fun.

Whether you're a meat eater, a vegetarian, or somewhere in the middle, you'll find plenty of inspiration to help you get started on your healthy eating path.

Let's delve into the realm of high-protein meals and see how they can keep you energized, healthy, and satisfied every day!

Table Content

20. Elf Sugar Cookie Bars

21. Santa's Belt Sugar Cookies

22. Holiday Sprinkle Donuts

23. Snowflake Cheese Quesadillas

24. Gingerbread Man Pizza Bites

25. Peppermint Hot Chocolate Bombs

26. Christmas Tree Veggie Platter

27. Santa's Reindeer Chow Mix

28. Chocolate Reindeer Noses

29. Elf Doughnut Holes

30. Grinch Punch

31. Frosty's Fruit Kabobs

32. Holiday Cranberry Bliss Bars

33. Christmas Tree Shaped Sandwiches

34. Rudolph's Red Velvet Cupcakes

35. Peppermint Bark Pretzels

36. Christmas Ornament Popcorn Balls

37. Santa's Reindeer Carrot Smoothie

38. Sugar Plum Fairy Fruit Salad

39. Elf-Sized Gingerbread Houses

40. Jolly Gingerbread Cupcakes

41. Peppermint Patty Snowballs

42. Snowman Cheese Ball

43. Grinch Green Smoothie

44. Santa's Stovetop S'mores

45. Reindeer Trail Mix

46. Holiday Cinnamon Roll Christmas Trees

47. Red and Green Cookie Pops

48. Santa's Beard Banana Bites

49. Gingerbread Pancakes with Whipped Cream

50. Christmas Tree Brownie Bites

1.Santa's Snowflake Pancakes

Fluffy pancakes with powdered sugar snowflakes.

Ingredients:

- 1 ½ cups all-purpose flour

- 1 tablespoon sugar

- 1 tablespoon baking powder

- ½ teaspoon salt

- 1 ¼ cups milk

- 1 large egg

- 3 tablespoons melted butter (plus extra for greasing)

- Powdered sugar (for dusting)

- Blueberries, strawberries, or sprinkles (optional for decoration)

- Whipped cream (optional)

Equipment:

- Snowflake pancake mold (optional)

- Squeeze bottle or piping bag (optional for snowflake design)

Instructions

1. **Prepare the dry ingredients:**

In a large bowl, whisk together the flour, sugar, baking powder, and salt until combined.

2. **Mix the wet ingredients:**

In another bowl, whisk together the milk, egg, and melted butter until smooth.

3. **Combine:**

Slowly add the wet ingredients to the dry ingredients and mix until just combined. Be careful not to overmix; lumps are okay.

4. **Preheat the pan:**

Heat a non-stick pan or griddle over medium heat. Lightly grease it with butter.

5. **Create the snowflake design:**

- With a mold: If you have a snowflake-shaped pancake mold, grease the mold and place it on the pan. Pour the pancake batter into the mold and cook until bubbles form on the surface (about 2 minutes), then remove the mold and flip the pancake, cooking for another minute or until golden brown.

- Without a mold: If you're feeling creative, you can pour the batter into a squeeze bottle or piping bag with a small tip, then pipe out a snowflake pattern directly onto the pan. This may take some practice but gives a unique snowflake look!

5. Cook pancakes:

Cook each pancake until bubbles form on the surface and the edges are set (around 2 minutes). Flip and cook the other side for another 1-2 minutes or until golden brown.

6. Serve:

Stack the pancakes on a plate and dust generously with powdered sugar to give the look of snowflakes. Add whipped cream, fresh blueberries, strawberries, or sprinkles for festive decoration.

7. Enjoy:

Serve warm with syrup on the side or a sprinkle of extra powdered sugar for a snowy effect!

2.Rudolph's Red Nose Pizza

Mini pizzas with red tomato "nose" and holiday toppings.

Ingredients:

- 1 ready-made pizza dough (or homemade)

- ½ cup pizza sauce

- 1 ½ cups shredded mozzarella cheese

- 10-12 slices of pepperoni

- 1 large slice of red bell pepper (for Rudolph's nose)

- 2 black olives (for eyes)

- 1 slice of mozzarella cheese (for eyes)

- Fresh basil leaves (optional, for garnish)

- Olive oil (for brushing)

- Cornmeal (for dusting)

Instructions:

1. Preheat the oven:

Preheat your oven to 220°C (425°F). If you're using a pizza stone, place it in the oven while it heats up. If not, prepare a baking sheet with a light dusting of cornmeal to prevent sticking.

2. Prepare the dough:

Roll out the pizza dough into a large round shape for the base of Rudolph's face. If you want a perfect circle, you can trim the edges slightly.

3. Add the sauce:

Spread an even layer of pizza sauce over the dough, leaving about a 1-2 cm (½ inch) border around the edges for the crust.

4. Add the cheese:

Sprinkle the shredded mozzarella cheese generously over the sauce, making sure it's evenly distributed.

5. Create Rudolph's face:

  - For the eyes: Cut two small circles from the slice of mozzarella cheese. Place them about 2-3 inches apart on the top half of the pizza to form Rudolph's eyes. Place a slice of black olive on each mozzarella circle for the pupils.

  - For the nose: Place a large red bell pepper slice in the center lower half of the pizza to create Rudolph's red nose.

  - For the antlers: Arrange pepperoni slices in an arched pattern on the upper part of the pizza to resemble Rudolph's antlers. You can even cut the pepperoni into strips to create a more realistic antler shape.

6. Bake the pizza:

Brush the edges of the dough with olive oil for a golden crust. Place the pizza on the prepared baking sheet (or pizza stone) and bake for 12-15 minutes or until the crust is golden and the cheese is bubbly and melted.

7.Garnish and serve:

 Remove the pizza from the oven and let it cool slightly. Garnish with fresh basil leaves if desired for a pop of green. Slice and enjoy your festive Rudolph's Red Nose Pizza!

This cute and fun pizza will be a hit at Christmas parties, especially with kids! It's easy to make and gives Rudolph's iconic red nose a delicious twist!

3. Frosty the Snowman Cookies

Snowman-shaped sugar cookies with frosty decorations.

Ingredients:

- 2 ¾ cups all-purpose flour

- 1 teaspoon baking soda

- ½ teaspoon baking powder

- 1 cup unsalted butter (softened)

- 1 ½ cups granulated sugar

- 1 large egg

- 1 teaspoon vanilla extract

- 3 tablespoons milk

- 1 cup white icing (store-bought or homemade)

- Mini marshmallows (for the head)

- Orange candy-coated chocolates or orange icing (for the nose)

- Mini chocolate chips (for the eyes and buttons)

- Pretzel sticks (for arms)

- Red and green sprinkles (optional for scarf and decoration)

Instructions:

1. **Preheat the oven:**

Preheat your oven to 175°C (350°F). Line a baking sheet with parchment paper or a silicone baking mat.

2. **Mix the dry ingredients:**

In a medium-sized bowl, whisk together the flour, baking soda, and baking powder. Set aside.

3. **Cream the butter and sugar:**

In a large bowl, beat the softened butter and sugar together until light and fluffy (about 2-3 minutes).

4. **Add wet ingredients:**

Add the egg, vanilla extract, and milk to the butter-sugar mixture. Beat until well combined.

5. **Combine ingredients:**

Gradually add the dry ingredients to the wet mixture, stirring until a soft dough forms.

6. Shape the cookies:

Using a tablespoon, scoop out dough and roll it into small balls. Place two dough balls side by side on the baking sheet (one slightly smaller for the head and one larger for the body). Gently press them together to create the snowman shape. Repeat with the remaining dough.

7. Bake the cookies:

Bake for 8-10 minutes, or until the edges are lightly golden but the centers remain soft. Allow the cookies to cool on the baking sheet for 2 minutes before transferring them to a wire rack to cool completely.

8. Decorate Frosty:

- Head:

Use a dollop of white icing to stick a mini marshmallow on top of the smaller cookie ball (the head).

- Nose:

Press an orange candy-coated chocolate into the marshmallow for Frosty's carrot nose. Alternatively, you can use orange icing to pipe a small nose.

- Eyes and buttons:

Place two mini chocolate chips on the marshmallow for Frosty's eyes. Use additional mini chocolate chips to create buttons on the larger cookie (the body).

- Arms:

Stick two pretzel sticks into the sides of the larger cookie to represent Frosty's arms.

- Optional decoration:

Use red and green sprinkles or icing to create a scarf around Frosty's neck for a festive touch.

9.Let the icing set:

Allow the icing and decorations to set before serving.

These Frosty the Snowman Cookies are as fun to decorate as they are to eat! Perfect for a holiday activity with kids, these cookies bring the magic of Frosty to your kitchen.

4.Reindeer Carrot Cupcakes

Carrot cupcakes decorated with reindeer faces and pretzel antlers.

Ingredients for the Cupcakes:

- 1 ½ cups all-purpose flour

- 1 teaspoon baking powder

- ½ teaspoon baking soda

- ½ teaspoon cinnamon

- ¼ teaspoon nutmeg

- ¼ teaspoon salt

- 1 cup granulated sugar

- ½ cup vegetable oil

- 2 large eggs

- 1 teaspoon vanilla extract

- 1 ½ cups grated carrots (about 3 medium carrots)

- ½ cup crushed pineapple (drained)

- ½ cup chopped walnuts (optional)

Ingredients for the Frosting:

- 1 cup cream cheese (softened)

- ½ cup unsalted butter (softened)

- 2 ½ cups powdered sugar

- 1 teaspoon vanilla extract

- Pretzel twists (for antlers)

- Chocolate-covered candies (for eyes and noses – red for Rudolph's nose!)

- Mini marshmallows (for the muzzle)

Instructions:

1. **Preheat the oven:**

Preheat your oven to 180°C (350°F). Line a muffin tin with cupcake liners.

2. **Mix dry ingredients:**

In a medium bowl, whisk together the flour, baking powder, baking soda, cinnamon, nutmeg, and salt.

3. **Mix wet ingredients:

In a separate large bowl, beat the sugar, vegetable oil, eggs, and vanilla extract until smooth and well-combined.

4. **Add carrots and pineapple:**

Stir the grated carrots and crushed pineapple into the wet mixture. If you're adding chopped walnuts, fold them in at this stage.

5. **Combine:**

Gradually add the dry ingredients to the wet mixture, stirring until just combined. Do not overmix.

6. **Bake the cupcakes:**

Divide the batter evenly into the prepared cupcake liners. Bake for 18-22 minutes, or until a toothpick inserted into the center comes out clean. Let the cupcakes cool in the pan for 5 minutes, then transfer them to a wire rack to cool completely.

7. **Prepare the frosting:**

While the cupcakes are cooling, beat the cream cheese and softened butter together in a large bowl until smooth. Add the vanilla extract, then gradually mix in the powdered sugar until the frosting is creamy and smooth.

8. **Decorate the reindeer faces:**

   - **Frost the cupcakes:** Generously frost each cooled cupcake with the cream cheese frosting.

   - **Create the antlers:** Stick two pretzel twists into the top of each cupcake for the reindeer's antlers.

   - **Add the eyes:** Use two chocolate-covered candies for the eyes of each reindeer.

   - **Make the nose and muzzle:** Press a red candy-coated chocolate in the center for Rudolph's nose, or use a brown candy for the rest of the reindeer. Place a mini marshmallow just below the nose to form the muzzle.

9. **Serve:**

Allow the frosting to set slightly before serving your adorable Reindeer Carrot Cupcakes!

These festive Reindeer Carrot Cupcakes combine the sweetness of carrot cake with a holiday twist! Perfect for Christmas parties or as a fun baking activity with kids.

5. Christmas Tree Quesadillas

Cut the cheesy quesadillas into Christmas tree shapes.

Ingredients:

- 4 large spinach tortillas (for a green tree effect)

- 2 cups shredded cheddar cheese (or any cheese of choice)

- 1 cup cooked shredded chicken (optional)

- 1 small red bell pepper (for ornaments)

- 1 small yellow bell pepper (for the star)

- Sour cream (for snow)

- Salsa (for dipping)

- Guacamole (for added greenery)

Instructions:

1. **Preheat the skillet:**

Heat a non-stick skillet or griddle over medium heat.

2. **Assemble the quesadillas:**

Place one spinach tortilla on a clean surface. Sprinkle a layer of shredded cheese evenly over the tortilla, leaving a small border around the edge. If using chicken, evenly distribute it over the cheese.

3. **Top with another tortilla:**

Place a second spinach tortilla on top, pressing down lightly.

4. **Cook the quesadilla:**

Place the assembled quesadilla on the preheated skillet. Cook for 2-3 minutes on each side, or until the tortilla is golden and crispy, and the cheese has melted.

5. **Cut into triangles:**

Once the quesadilla is cooked, remove it from the skillet. Cut the quesadilla into triangles to mimic the shape of a Christmas tree.

6. **Decorate the tree:**

   - Ornaments:

Dice the red bell pepper into small pieces and sprinkle them on the quesadilla triangles to resemble ornaments.

   - Star:

Cut the yellow bell pepper into small star shapes (you can use a small star-shaped cookie cutter or a knife) and place one at the top of each quesadilla triangle as the tree topper.

7.Add snowy details:

Use a piping bag or spoon to add a drizzle of sour cream along the edges of the tree to resemble snow.

8.Serve:

Arrange the quesadilla trees on a platter with salsa and guacamole on the side for dipping.

6. Elf Hat Mini Pizzas

Mini pizzas styled like elf hats, with colorful toppings.

Ingredients:

- 1 package of pizza dough (store-bought or homemade)

- ½ cup pizza sauce

- 1 ½ cups shredded mozzarella cheese

- Pepperoni slices (or mini pepperoni)

- 1 small green bell pepper (for the hat trim)

- Cherry tomatoes (for the hat's pom-pom)

- Olive oil (for brushing)

- Cornmeal (for dusting)

- Fresh basil (optional, for garnish)

Instructions:

1. **Preheat the oven:**

Preheat your oven to 220°C (425°F). Line a baking sheet with parchment paper or lightly dust with cornmeal to prevent sticking.

2. **Roll out the dough:**

Roll out the pizza dough on a floured surface to about ¼-inch thickness. Use a triangle-shaped cookie cutter or a knife to cut the dough into small triangle shapes (these will resemble elf hats).

3. **Prepare the mini pizzas:**

Place the triangle-shaped dough pieces on the prepared baking sheet.

4. **Add the sauce:**

Spread a thin layer of pizza sauce over each triangle, leaving a small border around the edges.

5. **Top with cheese:**

Sprinkle a generous amount of shredded mozzarella cheese over the sauce on each mini pizza.

6. **Decorate the elf hats:**

- Hat trim:

Slice the green bell pepper into thin strips. Place one strip along the bottom of each triangle to create the trim of the elf hat.

- Pom-pom:

Place a cherry tomato at the top of each triangle to serve as the pom-pom of the hat.

7.Add pepperoni (optional):

If desired, place a few pepperoni slices on each mini pizza for extra flavor and decoration.

8.Bake the mini pizzas:

Brush the edges of the dough with olive oil to help them turn golden and crispy. Bake the mini pizzas for 10-12 minutes, or until the cheese is melted and bubbly, and the crust is golden brown.

9. Garnish and serve:

Remove the mini pizzas from the oven and let them cool for a minute. Garnish with fresh basil leaves if desired, and serve warm.

7. North Pole Hot Chocolate

Creamy hot chocolate with marshmallows and sprinkles.

Ingredients:

- 4 cups whole milk (or any milk of your choice)

- 1 cup heavy cream

- 1 cup semi-sweet chocolate chips

- ¼ cup cocoa powder

- ¼ cup sugar (adjust to taste)

- 1 teaspoon vanilla extract

- Whipped cream (for topping)

- Candy canes (for stirring)

- Mini marshmallows (optional)

- Red and green sprinkles (optional)

- Chocolate syrup (for drizzling)

- Crushed peppermint candies (optional, for garnish)

Instructions:

1. **Heat the milk and cream:**

In a medium saucepan, heat the milk and heavy cream over medium heat until warm but not boiling.

2. **Add the chocolate:**

Stir in the chocolate chips, cocoa powder, and sugar. Continue stirring until the chocolate chips are completely melted, and the mixture is smooth and creamy. Adjust the sugar to taste if you prefer a sweeter hot chocolate.

3. **Add vanilla:**

Stir in the vanilla extract and whisk the hot chocolate to ensure everything is well combined.

4. **Prepare the toppings:**

While the hot chocolate is heating, crush a few candy canes or peppermint candies if you want to use them for garnish. Get the whipped cream, sprinkles, mini marshmallows, and chocolate syrup ready.

5. **Serve the hot chocolate:**

Pour the hot chocolate into festive mugs. Top generously with whipped cream and a handful of mini marshmallows.

6. **Garnish:**

Drizzle chocolate syrup over the whipped cream, sprinkle with red and green sprinkles, and add a crushed candy cane or peppermint candy for a festive touch.

7. **Add a candy cane stirrer:**

Place a candy cane in each mug as a fun North Pole stirrer.

8. **Enjoy:**

Sip and enjoy your rich, decadent "North Pole Hot Chocolate", perfect for warming up during the holiday season!

8. Gingerbread Men Sandwiches

Delightful gingerbread-shaped sandwiches loaded with delicious goodies.

Ingredients for Gingerbread Cookies:

- 3 cups all-purpose flour

- 1 teaspoon baking soda

- 2 teaspoons ground ginger

- 1 teaspoon ground cinnamon

- ½ teaspoon ground nutmeg

- ¼ teaspoon ground cloves

- ¼ teaspoon salt

- ¾ cup unsalted butter (softened)

- ¾ cup brown sugar

- 1 large egg

- ½ cup molasses

- 1 teaspoon vanilla extract

Ingredients for Filling:

- 1 cup cream cheese (softened)

- ½ cup unsalted butter (softened)

- 2 cups powdered sugar

- 1 teaspoon vanilla extract

- ½ teaspoon ground cinnamon (optional)

Instructions:

1. **Prepare the gingerbread cookie dough:**

  - In a medium bowl, whisk together the flour, baking soda, ginger, cinnamon, nutmeg, cloves, and salt.

  - In a large bowl, cream the softened butter and brown sugar until light and fluffy. Add the egg, molasses, and vanilla extract, and beat until smooth.

  - Gradually add the dry ingredients to the wet ingredients, mixing until just combined.

  - Divide the dough in half, wrap each portion in plastic wrap, and chill in the fridge for at least 1 hour (or overnight).

2. **Preheat the oven:**

Preheat your oven to 180°C (350°F). Line two baking sheets with parchment paper.

3. Roll out and cut the cookies:

- On a floured surface, roll out the chilled dough to about ¼-inch thickness.

- Use a gingerbread man-shaped cookie cutter to cut out shapes from the dough. Place the cookies on the prepared baking sheets, spacing them about 1 inch apart.

4. Bake the cookies:

Bake for 8-10 minutes, or until the edges are firm and the cookies are slightly golden. Let them cool on the baking sheet for 5 minutes before transferring to a wire rack to cool completely.

5. Prepare the filling:

- While the cookies cool, prepare the cream cheese filling by beating the softened cream cheese and butter together in a large bowl until smooth.

- Add the powdered sugar, vanilla extract, and cinnamon (if using), and continue to beat until creamy and fluffy.

6. Assemble the gingerbread men sandwiches:

- Once the cookies have cooled completely, spread or pipe a generous amount of the cream cheese filling onto the flat side of one cookie.

- Top with another gingerbread cookie to create a sandwich. Repeat with the remaining cookies.

7. Decorate (optional):

- If you want to add a decorative touch, you can pipe icing or melted chocolate onto the gingerbread men or add sprinkles and mini candies for buttons and eyes.

8.Serve and enjoy:

These delightful Gingerbread Men Sandwiches are ready to enjoy!

9.Peppermint Candy Cane Milkshakes

Garnish peppermint shakes with candy cane bits.

Ingredients:

- 4 large scoops vanilla Ice cream

- 1 ½ cups whole milk (or any milk of your choice)

- 1 teaspoon peppermint extract

- 3 candy canes (crushed)

- Whipped cream (for topping)

- Red and green sprinkles (optional)

- Chocolate syrup (optional, for drizzling)

- Mini candy canes (for garnish)

Instructions:

1. **Crush the candy canes:**

Place the candy canes in a plastic bag and crush them with a rolling pin or heavy object until they are in small pieces but not too fine. Set aside.

2. **Blend the milkshake:**

In a blender, combine the vanilla ice cream, milk, peppermint extract, and about two-thirds of the crushed candy canes. Blend until smooth and creamy. If you prefer a thicker milkshake, add more ice cream. For a thinner shake, add a bit more milk.

3. **Prepare the glasses:**

Drizzle chocolate syrup along the inside of the glasses (optional for extra indulgence). You can also dip the rim of each glass in chocolate syrup and then coat with the remaining crushed candy canes for a festive touch.

4. **Serve the milkshake:**

Pour the peppermint milkshake into the prepared glasses.

5. **Add toppings:**

Top each milkshake with a generous swirl of whipped cream. Garnish with red and green sprinkles, more crushed candy canes, and a mini candy cane for decoration.

6. **Enjoy:**

Serve immediately with a straw and enjoy your refreshing Peppermint Candy Cane Milkshake!

9. Christmas Light Cupcake Cones

Cupcakes cooked in cones and decorated with holiday lights.

Ingredients:

- 12 flat-bottomed ice cream cones

- 1 box of vanilla cake mix (or homemade vanilla cupcake batter)

- 1 cup butter (softened)

- 4 cups powdered sugar

- 2-3 tablespoons milk

- 1 teaspoon vanilla extract

- Green food coloring

- Assorted colored candy-coated chocolates (for lights)

- Black licorice strips (for the string)

- Sprinkles (optional, for extra decoration)

Instructions:

1. **Preheat the oven:**

Preheat your oven to 180°C (350°F). Line a muffin tin with foil and place a flat-bottomed ice cream cone in each cup, standing upright.

2. **Prepare the cake batter:**

Prepare the vanilla cake mix according to the package instructions, or make your own homemade vanilla cupcake batter.

3. **Fill the cones:**

Carefully spoon the cake batter into the cones, filling each about ⅔ of the way. Be sure not to overfill, as the batter will rise during baking.

4. **Bake the cupcake cones:**

Bake in the preheated oven for 15-18 minutes, or until a toothpick inserted into the center of the cupcakes comes out clean. Allow them to cool completely.

5. **Make the frosting:**

In a large bowl, beat the softened butter until smooth. Gradually add the powdered sugar, milk, and vanilla extract, and beat until light and fluffy. Add a few drops of green food coloring and mix until the frosting is a vibrant green.

6. **Frost the cones:**

Once the cupcake cones are cool, use a piping bag or a spoon to generously frost the top of each cone with the green frosting to resemble a Christmas tree.

7. Decorate with lights:

   - Place small candy-coated chocolates around the frosted cone to resemble Christmas lights.

   - Use the black licorice strips to create a string effect by placing small pieces around the frosting, connecting the candy lights.

8.Add extra decorations (optional):

If desired, sprinkle additional sprinkles or edible glitter over the frosting for extra festive sparkle.

9.Serve and enjoy:

Your fun and festive Christmas Light Cupcake Cones are ready to serve! They make a perfect treat for kids and holiday gatherings.

10. Snowball Energy Bites

Coconut-covered energy nibbles are ideal for holiday snacking.

Ingredients:

- 1 cup rolled oats

- ½ cup almond butter (or peanut butter)

- ¼ cup honey or maple syrup

- ½ cup shredded coconut (plus extra for rolling)

- ¼ cup mini chocolate chips (optional)

- 1 teaspoon vanilla extract

- 1 tablespoon chia seeds (optional, for added texture and nutrition)

- 1 tablespoon flaxseed meal (optional)

- Pinch of salt

Instructions:

1. **Mix the dry ingredients:**

In a large mixing bowl, combine the rolled oats, shredded coconut, mini chocolate chips (if using), chia seeds, flaxseed meal, and a pinch of salt. Stir until evenly distributed.

2. **Add the wet ingredients:**

Add the almond butter, honey (or maple syrup), and vanilla extract to the dry mixture. Stir well until everything is fully combined, and the mixture sticks together.

3. **Chill the mixture:**

Place the mixture in the fridge for about 20-30 minutes. This makes it easier to roll into balls.

4. **Roll into snowballs:**

After chilling, take small portions of the mixture (about 1 tablespoon each) and roll them into bite-sized balls.

5. **Coat with coconut:**

Pour some extra shredded coconut onto a plate. Roll each energy bite in the coconut to coat, making them look like little snowballs.

6. **Store and serve:**

Place the "Snowball Energy Bites" in an airtight container and store in the refrigerator for up to 1 week. They can also be frozen for up to 3 months.

12. Jingle Bell Brownies

Holiday brownies topped with colorful sprinkles.

Ingredients for Brownies:

- 1 cup unsalted butter (melted)

- 1 cup granulated sugar

- 1 cup brown sugar (packed)

- 4 large eggs

- 1 teaspoon vanilla extract

- 1 cup all-purpose flour

- 1 cup cocoa powder

- ½ teaspoon salt

- 1 cup chocolate chips (optional)

Ingredients for Decoration:

- 1 ½ cups powdered sugar

- 2-3 tablespoons milk (for icing)

- Red and green food coloring

- Assorted colored candies or sprinkles (for jingle bells)

- Edible glitter (optional)

- Mini candy canes (optional, for garnish)

Instructions:

1. Preheat the oven:

Preheat your oven to 180°C (350°F). Line a 9x13-inch baking dish with parchment paper, leaving an overhang on the sides for easy removal.

2. Prepare the brownie batter:

- In a large bowl, whisk together the melted butter, granulated sugar, and brown sugar until smooth.

- Add the eggs, one at a time, mixing well after each addition. Stir in the vanilla extract.

- In a separate bowl, whisk together the flour, cocoa powder, and salt. Gradually add the dry ingredients to the wet mixture, stirring until just combined.

- Fold in the chocolate chips, if using.

3.Bake the brownies:

Pour the batter into the prepared baking dish and spread it evenly. Bake for 25-30 minutes, or until a toothpick inserted into the center comes out with a few moist crumbs. Allow the brownies to cool completely in the pan.

4.Make the icing:

While the brownies are cooling, prepare the icing by whisking the powdered sugar and milk together in a small bowl until smooth. If the icing is too thick, add a bit more milk,

1 teaspoon at a time. Divide the icing into two small bowls and tint one with red food coloring and the other with green.

5. Cut and decorate the brownies:

- Once the brownies are completely cool, lift them out of the pan using the parchment paper overhang. Cut the brownies into squares or festive shapes using cookie cutters (like stars or bells).

- Drizzle the red and green icing over the brownies to resemble jingle bell patterns. Alternatively, you can pipe the icing onto the brownies for more detailed designs.

- Add colored candies or sprinkles to represent the jingle bells. If desired, sprinkle with edible glitter for extra holiday sparkle.

6.Garnish and serve:

If using mini candy canes, press one into the top of each brownie for a fun garnish. Serve your "Jingle Bell Brownies" at your holiday party or as a festive treat for friends and family!

13. Santa's Hat Strawberry Treats

Fresh strawberries with whipped cream and chocolate.

Ingredients:

- 12 large strawberries (washed and dried)

- 1 cup whipped cream cheese (or regular cream cheese, softened)

- ¼ cup powdered sugar

- 1 teaspoon vanilla extract

- 12 mini marshmallows

- Red sugar sprinkles (optional, for decoration)

- Fresh mint leaves (optional, for garnish)

Instructions:

1. Prepare the cream cheese mixture:

   - In a medium bowl, beat the whipped cream cheese, powdered sugar, and vanilla extract together until smooth and fluffy. You can use a hand mixer or a whisk.

2. Prepare the strawberries:

   - If necessary, slice a tiny bit off the bottom of each strawberry to create a flat base, allowing them to stand upright. This will help the strawberries stay stable when assembled.

3. Fill the strawberries:

   - Using a piping bag or a small spoon, fill each strawberry with the cream cheese mixture, creating a dollop on top to resemble Santa's hat.

4. Add the marshmallows:

   - Place a mini marshmallow on top of each filled strawberry to represent the pom-pom on Santa's hat.

5. Decorate (optional):

   - If desired, sprinkle some red sugar sprinkles on the cream cheese filling to add a festive touch. You can also garnish the plate with fresh mint leaves for a pop of color.

6. Serve:

   - Arrange the Santa's Hat Strawberry Treats on a serving platter. Serve immediately or refrigerate for up to 1 hour before serving.

14. Candy Cane Pretzel Sticks

Pretzel sticks coated in chocolate and peppermint candy.

Ingredients:

- 1 bag of pretzel rods (about 12-15 pretzels)

- 1 cup white chocolate chips (or almond bark)

- ½ cup crushed candy canes (about 3-4 candy canes)

- Sprinkles (optional, for decoration)

- Wax paper (for cooling)

Instructions:

1. **Prepare the candy canes:**

Place the candy canes in a plastic bag and crush them into small pieces using a rolling pin or a heavy object. Set aside.

2. **Melt the chocolate:**

   - In a microwave-safe bowl, melt the white chocolate chips. Microwave in 30-second intervals, stirring in between, until the chocolate is completely melted and smooth. Be careful not to overheat it.

3. **Dip the pretzel rods:**

   - Dip each pretzel rod into the melted white chocolate, covering about two-thirds of the pretzel. Allow any excess chocolate to drip off.

4. **Coat with crushed candy canes:**

   - Immediately roll the chocolate-coated part of the pretzel in the crushed candy canes, ensuring an even coating. You can also sprinkle some crushed candy canes over the top for a more festive look.

5. **Add sprinkles (optional):**

   - If desired, sprinkle colorful holiday sprinkles on top of the melted chocolate before it sets.

6. **Cool the pretzels:**

   - Place the coated pretzel sticks on a sheet of wax paper to cool and harden. You can speed up the process by placing them in the refrigerator for about 10-15 minutes.

7. **Serve and enjoy:**

   - Once the chocolate has hardened, your "Candy Cane Pretzel Sticks" are ready to serve! They can be enjoyed immediately or stored in an airtight container at room temperature for up to a week.

15. Snowy White Chocolate Popcorn

Sweet white chocolate popcorn sprinkled with coconut.

Ingredients:

- 8 cups plain popped popcorn (about ½ cup unpopped kernels)

- 1 cup white chocolate chips (or white candy melts)

- ½ cup powdered sugar

- ½ teaspoon vanilla extract (optional)

- ¼ cup sprinkles (optional, for decoration)

- ½ cup mini marshmallows (optional)

1. Pop the popcorn:

   - Pop the popcorn using your preferred method (stovetop, air-popper, or microwave). Remove any unpopped kernels and place the popcorn in a large mixing bowl.

2. Melt the white chocolate:

   - In a microwave-safe bowl, melt the white chocolate chips or candy melts. Microwave in 30-second intervals, stirring in between until fully melted and smooth. If using, stir in the vanilla extract for added flavor.

3. Coat the popcorn:

   - Pour the melted white chocolate over the popcorn, gently tossing to coat the popcorn evenly. Use a spatula or your hands to make sure all the popcorn is covered.

4. Add powdered sugar:

   - While the white chocolate is still wet, sprinkle the powdered sugar over the popcorn and toss again to give it a snowy effect.

5. Decorate (optional):

   - If desired, sprinkle colorful holiday sprinkles or mini marshmallows over the coated popcorn for added fun and texture.

6. Cool the popcorn:

   - Spread the coated popcorn onto a large sheet of wax paper or parchment paper and allow it to cool for about 15-20 minutes until the chocolate hardens.

7. Serve and enjoy:

   - Once the white chocolate has set, your Snowy White Chocolate Popcorn is ready to serve! Store any leftovers in an airtight container at room temperature for up to 3 days.

16. Rudolph's Carrot Sticks with Dip

Carrot sticks with a creamy dip, reindeer style.

Ingredients for Carrot Sticks:

- 10-12 large carrots (peeled and cut into sticks)

- 1 tablespoon olive oil (optional, for roasting)

- Salt and pepper to taste (optional, for seasoning)

Ingredients for Dip:

- 1 cup Greek yogurt (or sour cream)

- 2 tablespoons fresh dill (chopped)

- 1 tablespoon lemon juice

- 1 garlic clove (minced)

- Salt and pepper to taste

- 1 tablespoon olive oil (optional, for added creaminess)

- Fresh chives or parsley (optional, for garnish)

Instructions:

1. Prepare the carrots:

  - Peel the carrots and cut them into long, thin sticks, about 3-4 inches in length. You can serve the carrot sticks raw or roasted.

  - "For roasted carrots:" Preheat your oven to 200°C (400°F). Toss the carrot sticks in olive oil, salt, and pepper, then spread them in a single layer on a baking sheet. Roast for 15-20 minutes, flipping halfway through, until tender and slightly caramelized. Allow them to cool.

2. Make the dip:

- In a small mixing bowl, combine the Greek yogurt, fresh dill, lemon juice, minced garlic, olive oil (if using), salt, and pepper. Stir until well mixed. Adjust the seasoning to taste.

- For extra flavor, garnish with chopped chives or parsley.

3. Assemble and serve:

- Arrange the carrot sticks in a serving dish or platter. Serve the dip in a small bowl alongside the carrots.

- For a festive Rudolph-themed presentation, you can arrange the carrot sticks to resemble reindeer antlers around the dip.

4. Enjoy:

Your "Rudolph's Carrot Sticks with Dip" are ready to be enjoyed as a healthy, fun holiday snack!

These "Rudolph's Carrot Sticks with Dip" are a simple and nutritious holiday treat perfect for kids and adults alike. Whether raw or roasted, the carrots pair wonderfully with the creamy, herb-infused yogurt dip, making them a refreshing addition to your Christmas spread!

17. Mistletoe Marshmallow Pops

Marshmallow pops with chocolate and sprinkles.

Ingredients:

- 12 large marshmallows

- 1 cup green candy melts (or chocolate melts)

- 1 cup white chocolate chips (optional, for drizzle)

- ½ cup crushed graham crackers (optional, for texture)

- Lollipop sticks or skewers

- Red candy melts (for decoration)

- Green sprinkles (for decoration)

- Edible glitter (optional, for festive sparkle)

Instructions:

1. Prepare the marshmallows:

   - Insert a lollipop stick or skewer into each marshmallow, making sure it goes in about halfway.

2. Melt the green candy melts:

   - In a microwave-safe bowl, melt the green candy melts in 30-second intervals, stirring in between until completely melted and smooth.

3. Dip the marshmallows:

   - Dip each marshmallow into the melted green candy, swirling it around to coat it evenly. Allow any excess to drip off.

4. Add toppings:

   - While the green candy coating is still wet, roll the coated marshmallow in crushed graham crackers for texture or sprinkle with green sprinkles for a festive look.

5. Melt the white chocolate (optional):

   - If desired, melt the white chocolate chips in a separate bowl. Drizzle the melted white chocolate over the green-coated marshmallows for an added decorative touch.

6. Decorate with red:

   - Melt the red candy melts in a microwave-safe bowl and use a small piping bag or a fork to drizzle the red candy over the green marshmallows to resemble holly berries.

7. Cool the pops:

   - Place the marshmallow pops upright in a glass or styrofoam block to allow them to cool and harden completely. If desired, you can also place them in the refrigerator for about 15-20 minutes to set.

8. Add final touches (optional):

   - If using edible glitter, sprinkle it over the marshmallow pops for a sparkling effect before they fully set.

9. Serve and enjoy:

   - Your Mistletoe Marshmallow Pops are now ready to be enjoyed! These festive treats make perfect gifts, party favors, or delightful additions to your holiday dessert table.

18. Polar Bear Pudding Cups

Vanilla pudding cups decorated with marshmallow polar bears.

*

Ingredients:

- 2 cups vanilla pudding (store-bought or homemade)

- 1 cup whipped cream

- 12 mini chocolate chips (for eyes)

- 6 large marshmallows (for snouts)

- 6 small chocolate buttons or chocolate chips (for noses)

- 12 mini marshmallows (for ears)

- 6 small clear cups (for serving)

Instructions:

1. **Prepare the pudding:**

  - If you're making homemade vanilla pudding, prepare it in advance and allow it to cool. Alternatively, use store-bought vanilla pudding for convenience.

  - Spoon the vanilla pudding evenly into 6 small clear cups, filling each about ¾ of the way.

2. **Top with whipped cream:**

  - Add a generous layer of whipped cream on top of each pudding cup to create a snowy effect.

3. **Make the polar bear faces:**

  - "For the snouts:" Place a large marshmallow in the center of each whipped cream layer. Press a chocolate button or chocolate chip into the center of the marshmallow to create the polar bear's nose.

  - "For the eyes:" Place two mini chocolate chips above the marshmallow snout to form the polar bear's eyes.

  - "For the ears:" Use two mini marshmallows for each polar bear, placing them on top of the whipped cream on either side of the face to create ears.

4. **Decorate (optional):**

  - You can add more whipped cream around the edges or sprinkle some edible glitter on top to enhance the frosty, polar bear look.

5. **Chill and serve:**

  - Refrigerate the "Polar Bear Pudding Cups" for about 15-20 minutes before serving, allowing the whipped cream to firm up slightly.

6. **Enjoy:**

  - Serve these adorable "Polar Bear Pudding Cups" as a fun and tasty holiday treat! They're perfect for kids' parties, Christmas gatherings, or as a playful dessert during the winter season.

19. Christmas Wreath Rice Krispies

Rice Krispie treats shaped like festive wreaths with sprinkles.

Ingredients:

- 6 cups Rice Krispies cereal

- 1 package (10 oz) mini marshmallows

- 3 tablespoons unsalted butter

- Green food coloring

- Red M&Ms or mini red candies (for decoration)

- Mini pretzels or licorice strings (for bows, optional)

- Cooking spray or butter (for greasing hands and tools)

Instructions:

1. **Melt the marshmallows and butter:**

  - In a large saucepan, melt the butter over low heat. Once melted, add the mini marshmallows, stirring constantly until fully melted and smooth.

2. **Add the green food coloring:**

  - Remove the saucepan from heat and add a few drops of green food coloring. Stir well until the marshmallow mixture is evenly colored. Add more food coloring if needed to achieve a vibrant green.

3. **Mix in the Rice Krispies:**

  - Gradually fold in the Rice Krispies cereal, stirring until the cereal is fully coated with the green marshmallow mixture.

4. **Shape the wreaths:**

  - Grease your hands lightly with cooking spray or butter to prevent sticking. Take small handfuls of the mixture and form them into individual wreath shapes by creating a circle with a hole in the middle. You can also press the mixture into a greased donut pan to shape them uniformly.

5. **Decorate the wreaths:**

  - While the wreaths are still sticky, press red M&Ms or mini red candies into each wreath to resemble holly berries. For added decoration, use mini pretzels or licorice strings to form bows and place them at the bottom of each wreath.

6. **Allow to set:**

  - Place the Christmas Wreath Rice Krispies on a sheet of wax paper and let them set at room temperature for about 30 minutes until firm.

7. **Serve and enjoy:**

  - Once set, your Christmas Wreath Rice Krispies are ready to be served! They can be stored in an airtight container at room temperature for up to 3 days.

20. Elf Sugar Cookie Bars

Soft sugar cookie bars with festive elf hues.

Ingredients:

- **For the Cookie Bars:**

- 1 cup (225g) unsalted butter, softened

- 1 cup (200g) granulated sugar

- 1 large egg

- 1 teaspoon vanilla extract

- 1/2 teaspoon almond extract (optional)

- 2 1/4 cups (280g) all-purpose flour

- 1/2 teaspoon baking powder

- 1/4 teaspoon salt

- 1/4 cup festive sprinkles (red, green, white)

For the Frosting:

- 1/2 cup (115g) unsalted butter, softened

- 3 cups (360g) powdered sugar

- 2 tablespoons milk

- 1 teaspoon vanilla extract

- Food coloring (red, green, optional)

- Extra festive sprinkles for decoration

Instructions:

1. Preheat the Oven:

 - Preheat your oven to 350°F (180°C) and line a 9x13-inch baking pan with parchment paper or lightly grease it.

2. Make the Cookie Dough:

 - In a large mixing bowl, cream together the softened butter and granulated sugar until light and fluffy, about 2-3 minutes.

 - Add the egg, vanilla extract, and almond extract (if using). Mix until well combined.

 - In a separate bowl, whisk together the flour, baking powder, and salt.

 - Gradually add the dry ingredients to the butter mixture, mixing until a soft dough forms.

 - Gently fold in the sprinkles, ensuring they are evenly distributed throughout the dough.

3. **Bake the Cookie Bars:**

 - Press the dough evenly into the prepared baking pan, smoothing the top with a spatula or your hands.

 - Bake for 20-25 minutes, or until the edges are lightly golden and the center is set.

 - Remove from the oven and allow the bars to cool completely in the pan.

4. **Prepare the Frosting:**

 - While the cookie bars cool, prepare the frosting. In a large bowl, beat the softened butter until smooth and creamy.

 - Gradually add the powdered sugar, one cup at a time, mixing on low speed to avoid a sugar cloud.

 - Add the milk and vanilla extract, and increase the speed to medium-high, beating until the frosting is light and fluffy.

 - If desired, divide the frosting into separate bowls and tint with food coloring to create festive red and green frosting.

5. **Decorate the Bars:**

 - Once the cookie bars are completely cool, spread the frosting evenly over the top.

 - Add extra sprinkles for decoration, pressing them gently into the frosting to adhere.

6. **Cut and Serve:**

 - Cut into squares or rectangles, and serve your Elf Sugar Cookie Bars! Perfect for a holiday party or a Christmas treat.

21.Santa's Belt Sugar Cookies Recipe

Sugar cookies fashioned to resemble Santa's distinctive belt.

Ingredients:

For the Cookies:

- 1 cup (225g) unsalted butter, softened

- 1 cup (200g) granulated sugar

- 1 large egg

- 1 teaspoon vanilla extract

- 1/2 teaspoon almond extract (optional)

- 2 1/2 cups (310g) all-purpose flour

- 1/2 teaspoon baking powder

- 1/4 teaspoon salt

- Red gel food coloring

For the Royal Icing:

- 2 cups (240g) powdered sugar

- 2 tablespoons meringue powder

- 4 tablespoons water (add more if needed for desired consistency)

- Black gel food coloring

- Yellow gel food coloring

Instructions:

1. **Preheat the Oven:**

   - Preheat your oven to 350°F (180°C) and line a baking sheet with parchment paper.

2. **Prepare the Cookie Dough:**

   - In a large mixing bowl, cream together the softened butter and granulated sugar until light and fluffy, about 2-3 minutes.

   - Add the egg, vanilla extract, and almond extract (if using), and mix until well combined.

   - In a separate bowl, whisk together the flour, baking powder, and salt.

   - Gradually add the dry ingredients to the butter mixture, mixing until a soft dough forms.

   - Add the red gel food coloring to the dough, mixing until the dough is evenly colored.

3. **Chill the Dough:**

   - Form the dough into a ball, wrap it in plastic wrap, and chill in the fridge for at least 30 minutes. Chilling helps the cookies hold their shape while baking.

4. **Roll and Cut the Cookies:**

   - After chilling, roll the dough out on a lightly floured surface to about 1/4-inch thickness.

   - Use a round cookie cutter (about 3 inches in diameter) to cut out circles from the dough and place them on the prepared baking sheet.

   - Bake for 10-12 minutes, or until the edges are just lightly golden.

   - Remove from the oven and allow the cookies to cool completely on a wire rack.

5. **Prepare the Royal Icing:**

   - While the cookies cool, prepare the royal icing. In a medium bowl, whisk together the powdered sugar, meringue powder, and water. Adjust the water as needed to achieve a thick but spreadable consistency.

   - Divide the icing into two bowls. Tint one portion black for Santa's belt and the other yellow for the belt buckle.

6. **Decorate the Cookies:**

   - Once the cookies are cool, use the black icing to pipe a thick horizontal stripe across the center of each cookie, resembling Santa's belt.

   - Use the yellow icing to pipe a small square or rectangle in the middle of the black stripe to create Santa's belt buckle.

7. **Let the Icing Set:**

   - Allow the icing to set for at least 1-2 hours, or until fully dry, before serving or packaging the cookies.

22. Holiday Sprinkle Donuts

Fluffy donuts with beautiful holiday sprinkles.

Ingredients:

For the Donuts:

- 1 1/2 cups (190g) all-purpose flour

- 1/2 cup (100g) granulated sugar

- 1 1/2 teaspoons baking powder

- 1/4 teaspoon baking soda

- 1/4 teaspoon salt

- 1/2 teaspoon ground nutmeg (optional)

- 1/2 cup (120ml) milk

- 1/4 cup (60g) unsalted butter, melted

- 1 large egg

- 1 teaspoon vanilla extract

- 1/4 cup festive sprinkles (red, green, white)

For the Glaze:

- 1 cup (120g) powdered sugar

- 2 tablespoons milk

- 1/2 teaspoon vanilla extract

- Red and green food coloring (optional)

- Extra holiday sprinkles for topping

Instructions:

1. **Preheat the Oven:**

   - Preheat your oven to 350°F (180°C) and grease a donut pan with cooking spray or butter.

2. **Make the Donut Batter:**

   - In a large bowl, whisk together the flour, granulated sugar, baking powder, baking soda, salt, and nutmeg (if using).

- In a separate bowl, whisk the milk, melted butter, egg, and vanilla extract until combined.

- Gradually add the wet ingredients to the dry ingredients, stirring gently until a smooth batter forms. Be careful not to overmix.

- Fold in the festive sprinkles, mixing them evenly throughout the batter.

3. Fill the Donut Pan:

- Spoon the batter into the prepared donut pan, filling each cavity about 2/3 full. You can also use a piping bag for easier filling.

4. Bake the Donuts:

- Bake the donuts in the preheated oven for 10-12 minutes, or until they are lightly golden and a toothpick inserted into the center comes out clean.

- Remove the donuts from the oven and let them cool in the pan for 5 minutes, then transfer them to a wire rack to cool completely.

5. Prepare the Glaze:

- While the donuts cool, make the glaze by whisking together the powdered sugar, milk, and vanilla extract in a medium bowl until smooth.

- If desired, divide the glaze into two bowls and tint with red and green food coloring to match the holiday theme.

6. Glaze and Decorate the Donuts:

- Once the donuts are completely cool, dip the tops of each donut into the glaze, allowing any excess to drip off.

- Immediately sprinkle extra holiday sprinkles over the glazed donuts to add festive decoration.

- Allow the glaze to set for 15-20 minutes before serving.

These "Holiday Sprinkle Donuts" are perfect for a festive breakfast or a holiday treat to share with family and friends!

23. Snowflake Cheese Quesadillas

Crispy quesadillas cut into snowflake shapes.

Ingredients:

- 4 large flour tortillas

- 2 cups shredded cheese (cheddar, mozzarella, or a mix)

- 1 tablespoon butter or olive oil (for cooking)

- Optional fillings:

  - Sliced cooked chicken or turkey

- Sliced bell peppers

- Diced tomatoes

- Salsa or guacamole for serving

Instructions:

1. Prepare the Tortillas:

- Take two tortillas and fold them gently in half. Using clean kitchen scissors or a small knife, carefully cut out snowflake shapes or patterns along the folded edge, much like you would when making paper snowflakes. Unfold the tortillas to reveal the cut-out snowflake design.

2. Assemble the Quesadillas:

- Heat a non-stick skillet over medium heat. Add a small amount of butter or oil to the pan.

- Place one uncut tortilla on the skillet and sprinkle about 1/2 cup of shredded cheese evenly across the surface. If desired, add extra fillings like cooked chicken, bell peppers, or tomatoes on top of the cheese.

3. Top with the Snowflake Tortilla:

- Place one of the cut-out snowflake tortillas on top of the cheese layer. Press down gently to help the cheese melt and adhere the tortillas together.

4. Cook the Quesadilla:

- Cook for 2-3 minutes on each side, until the bottom tortilla is golden brown and the cheese is melted.

- Flip the quesadilla carefully using a spatula and cook the other side until it is also golden and crisp, about 2 more minutes.

5. Repeat with Remaining Tortillas:

- Repeat the process with the remaining tortillas and cheese to make more snowflake quesadillas.

6. Serve:

- Slice the quesadillas into wedges and serve with salsa, guacamole, or sour cream on the side for dipping.

These "Snowflake Cheese Quesadillas" are a fun and festive holiday snack or meal, perfect for kids and adults alike!

24. Gingerbread Man Pizza Bites

Mini pizzas with a gingerbread man twist.

Ingredients:

- 1 package pizza dough (store-bought or homemade)

- 1/2 cup pizza sauce

- 1 1/2 cups shredded mozzarella cheese

- Pepperoni slices, cut into small pieces (optional)

- Black olives, cut into small pieces (optional)

- Bell peppers, diced (optional)

- 1 tablespoon olive oil (for brushing)

- Gingerbread man cookie cutter

Instructions:

1. Preheat the Oven:

   - Preheat your oven to 400°F (200°C) and line a baking sheet with parchment paper.

2. Prepare the Pizza Dough:

   - Roll out the pizza dough on a lightly floured surface to about 1/4-inch thickness.

   - Use a gingerbread man cookie cutter to cut out as many shapes as possible from the dough. Gather the dough scraps, roll them out again, and continue cutting until you've used up the dough.

3. Assemble the Pizza Bites:

   - Place the gingerbread-shaped dough cutouts on the prepared baking sheet.

   - Spread a thin layer of pizza sauce over each gingerbread man, leaving a small border around the edges.

   - Sprinkle shredded mozzarella cheese over the sauce, covering the pizza.

4. Add the Toppings:

- Decorate each gingerbread man pizza with small pieces of pepperoni, black olives, and diced bell peppers to create eyes, buttons, and mouths. You can get creative with the placement to make fun and festive pizza bites.

5. Bake the Pizza Bites:

   - Lightly brush the edges of the dough with olive oil for a golden finish.

   - Bake in the preheated oven for 10-12 minutes, or until the cheese is melted and bubbly, and the edges of the dough are golden brown.

6. Serve:

   - Remove the pizza bites from the oven and let them cool slightly before serving. These "Gingerbread Man Pizza Bites" are perfect as a fun holiday snack or appetizer!

25. Peppermint Hot Chocolate Bombs

Chocolate bombs loaded with peppermint cocoa mixture.

Ingredients:

- 2 cups semi-sweet or milk chocolate chips (or melting chocolate)

- 1/2 cup hot chocolate mix

- 1/2 cup mini marshmallows

- 1/4 cup crushed peppermint candies or candy canes

- 1/2 teaspoon peppermint extract (optional)

- Silicone sphere molds (2-inch diameter)

- White chocolate chips or candy melts (optional for decoration)

Instructions:

1. **Melt the Chocolate:**

   - In a microwave-safe bowl, melt the chocolate chips in 20-second increments, stirring between each interval until fully melted and smooth.

   - If using peppermint extract, stir it into the melted chocolate for an extra minty flavor.

2. **Coat the Molds:**

   - Using a spoon or pastry brush, spread a thin layer of melted chocolate inside each cavity of the silicone sphere molds, making sure the sides are fully covered.

   - Place the molds in the refrigerator for 10 minutes to set.

   - Apply a second layer of chocolate to reinforce the sides of the molds, then refrigerate again for 10-15 minutes until completely hardened.

3. **Remove the Chocolate Shells:**

   - Gently pop the hardened chocolate shells out of the molds, being careful not to break them.

4. **Assemble the Hot Chocolate Bombs:**

   - Fill half of the chocolate shells with 1 tablespoon of hot chocolate mix, a few mini marshmallows, and a pinch of crushed peppermint candies.

   - Heat a plate in the microwave for 30 seconds, then place an empty chocolate shell on the warm plate for a few seconds to melt the edges slightly.

   - Quickly press the melted edge of the empty shell onto a filled shell to seal them together, creating a complete sphere. Repeat with all the chocolate bombs.

5. Decorate the Bombs:

   - Melt white chocolate chips or candy melts in the microwave and drizzle over the hot chocolate bombs for decoration.

- Sprinkle more crushed peppermint candies on top for a festive touch.

6. Serve:

- To enjoy, place a peppermint hot chocolate bomb in a mug and pour 1 cup of hot milk over it. Watch as the bomb melts, releasing the hot chocolate mix and marshmallows. Stir well and enjoy!

These Peppermint Hot Chocolate Bombs are a fun and festive way to enjoy a cozy holiday drink, perfect for gifting or sharing with friends and family!

26. Christmas Tree Veggie Platter

A vegetable tray made to resemble a Christmas tree.

Ingredients:

- 1 head of broccoli (for the tree)

- 1 cucumber (sliced)

- 1 pint cherry tomatoes

- 1 yellow bell pepper

- 1 red bell pepper

- 1/2 cup baby carrots

- 1/2 cup cauliflower florets (for the "snow")

- Fresh parsley or cilantro (for garnish)

- Star-shaped cookie cutter (for bell pepper star)

- 1 cup hummus, ranch dip, or your favorite dip (for serving)

Instructions:

1. Prepare the Vegetables:

   - Wash and chop the broccoli into small, bite-sized florets.

   - Slice the cucumber into thin rounds.

   - Halve the cherry tomatoes.

   - Cut the yellow and red bell peppers into strips, reserving a section of the yellow bell pepper to cut a star using the cookie cutter.

2. Assemble the Tree:

   - On a large platter or serving tray, start by creating the Christmas tree shape using the broccoli florets as the base. Arrange the florets in a wide triangle, making the tree's shape.

   - Add a layer of cucumber slices at the bottom to form the "tree trunk."

3. Decorate the Tree:

   - Use the cherry tomatoes as ornaments by scattering them across the broccoli tree.

   - Place the red and yellow bell pepper strips as garlands, draping them over the broccoli.

   - Cut a star shape from the yellow bell pepper and place it at the top of the tree.

   - Arrange baby carrots and cauliflower florets around the base of the tree to resemble snow and presents.

4. Garnish and Serve:

   - Sprinkle some parsley or cilantro around the platter for a festive, green touch.

   - Serve the veggie platter with hummus, ranch dip, or your favorite dip on the side.

This "Christmas Tree Veggie Platter" is a fun and healthy way to bring festive cheer to your holiday table, perfect for parties or family gatherings!

27. Santa's Reindeer Chow Mix

A sweet and salty snack mixture for Santa's reindeer.

Ingredients:

- 6 cups rice cereal squares (like Chex)

- 1 cup semi-sweet chocolate chips

- 1/2 cup creamy peanut butter

- 1/4 cup butter

- 1 teaspoon vanilla extract

- 1 1/2 cups powdered sugar

- 1 cup red and green candy-coated chocolates (like M&M's)

- 1 cup mini pretzels

- 1/2 cup mini marshmallows

- 1/4 cup holiday sprinkles (optional)

Instructions:

1. **Melt the Chocolate and Peanut Butter:**

  - In a microwave-safe bowl, combine the chocolate chips, peanut butter, and butter. Microwave in 30-second intervals, stirring between each, until the mixture is fully melted and smooth.

  - Stir in the vanilla extract.

2. **Coat the Cereal:**

  - Place the rice cereal squares in a large mixing bowl. Pour the melted chocolate-peanut butter mixture over the cereal and gently stir until all the pieces are coated evenly.

3. **Add the Powdered Sugar:**

  - Transfer the chocolate-coated cereal to a large resealable plastic bag (or use a large mixing bowl with a lid). Add the powdered sugar to the bag, seal it, and shake vigorously until all the cereal pieces are coated with the sugar. If using a bowl, cover and shake the cereal until evenly coated.

4. **Combine the Mix:**

  - Pour the coated cereal into a large serving bowl. Add the candy-coated chocolates, mini pretzels, mini marshmallows, and holiday sprinkles (if using). Gently toss everything together until well mixed.

5. **Serve:**

  - Santa's Reindeer Chow Mix is ready to enjoy! Serve it in a festive bowl or package it in small holiday bags for gifting.

This "Santa's Reindeer Chow Mix" is the perfect sweet and salty holiday snack, great for parties or as a fun treat for Santa's reindeer!

28. Chocolate Reindeer Noses

Chocolate balls designed to resemble Rudolph's red nose.

Ingredients:

- 1 bag (about 12 oz) pretzel rounds (or pretzel twists)

- 1 bag (about 12 oz) milk chocolate candy melts or chocolate chips

- 1/2 cup red candy-coated chocolates (like red M&M's)

Instructions:

1. **Melt the Chocolate:**

   - In a microwave-safe bowl, melt the milk chocolate candy melts or chocolate chips in 20-second intervals, stirring between each, until fully melted and smooth.

2. **Dip the Pretzels:**

   - Line a baking sheet with parchment paper or wax paper.

   - Dip each pretzel round (or pretzel twist) into the melted chocolate, using a fork or dipping tool to fully coat the pretzel.

   - Tap off any excess chocolate and place the dipped pretzel on the prepared baking sheet.

3. **Add the Reindeer Nose:**

   - Immediately press one red candy-coated chocolate (M&M) onto the center of each chocolate-dipped pretzel to create the reindeer's nose.

4. **Let the Chocolate Set:**

   - Allow the chocolate to set at room temperature for about 30 minutes or until hardened. If you want to speed up the process, place the baking sheet in the refrigerator for 10-15 minutes.

5. **Serve or Package:**

   - Once the chocolate has fully set, your "Chocolate Reindeer Noses" are ready to enjoy! Serve them in a festive bowl or package them in small holiday treat bags for gifting.

29. Elf Doughnut Holes

Mini doughnut holes with elf-themed decorations.

Ingredients:

- 1 can (16 oz) refrigerated biscuit dough (like Pillsbury Grands)

- 1 cup granulated sugar

- 1 tablespoon ground cinnamon

- 1 cup powdered sugar

- 2-3 tablespoons milk

- 1 teaspoon vanilla extract

- Vegetable oil (for frying)

- Red and green sprinkles (optional for decoration)

Instructions:

1. **Prepare the Cinnamon-Sugar Mixture:**

   - In a shallow bowl, combine the granulated sugar and ground cinnamon. Set aside.

2. **Prepare the Glaze:**

   - In a separate bowl, whisk together the powdered sugar, milk, and vanilla extract until smooth. If the glaze is too thick, add a little more milk until it reaches the desired consistency.

3. **Shape the Doughnut Holes:**

   - Open the can of biscuit dough and cut each biscuit into quarters. Roll each quarter into a small ball to form the doughnut holes.

4. **Heat the Oil:**

   - Pour about 2 inches of vegetable oil into a deep skillet or pot. Heat the oil over medium heat until it reaches 350°F (175°C). You can check the temperature using a candy thermometer, or test by dropping a small piece of dough into the oil—it should sizzle and rise to the surface.

5. **Fry the Doughnut Holes:**

   - Carefully drop a few doughnut holes into the hot oil, frying them in batches to avoid overcrowding. Fry for about 1-2 minutes on each side, or until golden brown and puffed up.

   - Remove the doughnut holes from the oil using a slotted spoon and place them on a paper towel-lined plate to drain excess oil.

6. Coat or Glaze the Doughnut Holes:

   - While the doughnut holes are still warm, roll half of them in the cinnamon-sugar mixture until fully coated.

   - Dip the other half in the prepared glaze, letting any excess drip off, and place them on a wire rack. If you like, sprinkle the glazed doughnut holes with red and green sprinkles for a festive touch.

7. Serve:

   - Once all the doughnut holes are coated or glazed, they're ready to serve! Enjoy them warm for the best taste.

These "Elf Doughnut Holes" are a fun, bite-sized treat perfect for holiday breakfasts, snacks, or parties!

30. Grinch Punch

A festive green punch inspired by The Grinch, ideal for parties.

Ingredients:

- 1 packet lime-flavored drink mix (like Kool-Aid or similar)

- 1 liter lemon-lime soda (like Sprite or 7-Up)

- 1 cup pineapple juice

- 1-2 cups vanilla ice cream

- Red sugar crystals (for rimming the glasses, optional)

- Red heart-shaped candies (optional for decoration)

Instructions:

1. Prepare the Glasses:

- If you want to make the presentation festive, dip the rims of your glasses in water and then into red sugar crystals to create a decorative sugared rim. Set the glasses aside.

2. Mix the Punch:

- In a large punch bowl, combine the lime-flavored drink mix with the lemon-lime soda and pineapple juice. Stir gently until everything is well mixed.

3. Add Ice Cream:

- Add scoops of vanilla ice cream to the punch mixture. The ice cream will float on top and melt into the punch, adding a creamy texture and frothy appearance, perfect for a "Grinchy" look.

4. Serve:

- Ladle the punch into the prepared glasses. For a fun touch, drop a red heart-shaped candy into each glass to represent the Grinch's growing heart.

This "Grinch Punch" is a fun, bright green drink that's perfect for holiday parties or family gatherings, adding a whimsical and festive touch to your Christmas celebration!

31. Frosty's Fruit Kabobs

Fruit skewers with a festive snowman theme.

Ingredients:

- 1 pint strawberries, hulled

- 1 cup green grapes

- 1 cup red grapes

- 2 bananas, sliced into rounds

- 1 pineapple, cut into chunks

- 1/2 cup mini marshmallows

- Wooden or plastic skewers

Instructions:

1. Prepare the Fruit:

   - Wash and dry the strawberries, grapes, and pineapple chunks.

   - Hull the strawberries by removing the leafy tops.

   - Slice the bananas into rounds and keep them in lemon water (a mix of water and lemon juice) to prevent browning, then drain before assembling.

2. Assemble the Kabobs:

   - Start threading the fruit onto the skewers in any desired pattern. For a festive look, alternate the colors of the fruit to create a Christmas-themed arrangement:

   - Start with a strawberry (as Frosty's "hat").

   - Add a banana slice.

   - Thread a chunk of pineapple.

   - Follow with a green grape, red grape, and mini marshmallow (for the snowball).

   - Repeat the pattern for the rest of the skewers.

3. Serve:

   - Arrange the finished fruit kabobs on a festive serving platter. Serve immediately for the best freshness, or store in the refrigerator until ready to serve.

These "Frosty's Fruit Kabobs" are a fun, healthy, and colorful snack, perfect for holiday parties or as a festive treat for kids!

32. Holiday Cranberry Bliss Bars

Cranberry-studded bars with a festive cream cheese icing.

Ingredients:

For the Bars:

- 1 cup unsalted butter, softened

- 1 cup brown sugar, packed

- 1/2 cup granulated sugar

- 2 large eggs

- 1 teaspoon vanilla extract

- 2 cups all-purpose flour

- 1 1/2 teaspoons baking powder

- 1/2 teaspoon ground ginger

- 1/2 teaspoon salt

- 1 cup white chocolate chips

- 3/4 cup dried cranberries

For the Frosting:

- 8 oz cream cheese, softened

- 1 cup powdered sugar

- 1 teaspoon vanilla extract

- 1/2 cup white chocolate chips, melted

For the Topping:

- 1/3 cup dried cranberries, chopped

- 1/4 cup white chocolate chips, melted (for drizzling)

Instructions:

1. **Preheat the Oven:**

   - Preheat your oven to 350°F (175°C). Line a 9x13-inch baking pan with parchment paper or lightly grease it.

2. **Make the Bar Batter:**

   In a large mixing bowl, cream together the softened butter, brown sugar, and granulated sugar until light and fluffy.

   - Beat in the eggs, one at a time, followed by the vanilla extract.

   - In a separate bowl, whisk together the flour, baking powder, ground ginger, and salt.

- Gradually add the dry ingredients to the wet ingredients, mixing until just combined.

- Stir in the white chocolate chips and dried cranberries.

3. Bake the Bars:

   - Spread the batter evenly into the prepared baking pan.

   - Bake for 18-22 minutes, or until a toothpick inserted into the center comes out clean, and the edges are golden brown.

   - Remove from the oven and let the bars cool completely in the pan.

4. Prepare the Frosting:

   - In a medium bowl, beat the softened cream cheese, powdered sugar, and vanilla extract until smooth and creamy.

   - Stir in the melted white chocolate until well combined.

5. Frost the Bars:

   - Once the bars are completely cool, spread the cream cheese frosting evenly over the top.

6. Add the Toppings:

   - Sprinkle the chopped dried cranberries evenly over the frosted bars.

   - Drizzle the melted white chocolate over the top for a decorative finish.

7. Chill and Cut:

   - Place the bars in the refrigerator for about 30 minutes to allow the frosting to set.

   - Once set, cut the bars into triangles or squares, and serve!

These "Holiday Cranberry Bliss Bars" are a sweet and tangy treat, perfect for sharing at Christmas parties or as a holiday dessert!

33. Christmas Tree Shaped Sandwiches

For some seasonal fun, make sandwiches in the shape of Christmas trees.

Ingredients:

- 8 slices of bread (white, whole wheat, or your choice)

- 4 tablespoons cream cheese or softened butter

- 4 slices ham, turkey, or deli meat of choice

- 4 slices cheddar or Swiss cheese

- 1 cucumber, thinly sliced (for decoration)

- 1 small red bell pepper, sliced into thin strips (for decoration)

- 1 small yellow bell pepper (optional, for star)

- Christmas tree-shaped cookie cutter

Instructions:

1. Prepare the Sandwich Base:

   - Lay out the slices of bread on a clean surface.

   - Using a Christmas tree-shaped cookie cutter, cut out tree shapes from each slice of bread. You can cut two trees from one slice if your cutter is small enough.

2. Assemble the Sandwiches:

   - Spread cream cheese or butter on half of the tree-shaped bread slices.

   - Place a slice of deli meat and a slice of cheese on top of the buttered/creamed bread.

   - Cover with another tree-shaped bread slice to make a sandwich.

3. Decorate the Sandwiches:

   - Use thin slices of cucumber and red bell pepper strips to create a garland or ornaments on the "tree."

   - Optionally, use a small star-shaped cutter to cut out a star from the yellow bell pepper and place it on top of each sandwich.

4. Serve:

   - Arrange the finished Christmas tree-shaped sandwiches on a festive platter and serve immediately.

These "Christmas Tree Shaped Sandwiches" are a fun, festive addition to any holiday gathering, perfect for kids and adults alike!

34. Rudolph's Red Velvet Cupcakes

Red velvet cupcakes with a reindeer motif.

Ingredients:

For the Cupcakes:

- 1 1/4 cups all-purpose flour

- 1 cup granulated sugar

- 1 tablespoon cocoa powder (unsweetened)

- 1/2 teaspoon baking soda

- 1/2 teaspoon salt

- 1 large egg

- 1/2 cup vegetable oil

- 1/2 cup buttermilk

- 1 tablespoon red food coloring

- 1 teaspoon vanilla extract

- 1 teaspoon white vinegar

For the Cream Cheese Frosting:

- 8 oz cream cheese, softened

- 1/4 cup unsalted butter, softened

- 2 cups powdered sugar

- 1 teaspoon vanilla extract

For Decorating:

- Mini pretzels (for antlers)

- Red candy (like M&M's or red gumdrops for the nose)

- Candy eyes (available in baking sections)

Instructions:

1. **Preheat the Oven:**

   - Preheat your oven to 350°F (175°C). Line a 12-cup muffin tin with cupcake liners.

2. **Make the Cupcakes:**

   - In a large bowl, whisk together the flour, sugar, cocoa powder, baking soda, and salt.

   - In another bowl, whisk the egg, vegetable oil, buttermilk, red food coloring, vanilla extract, and white vinegar until well combined.

   - Gradually add the wet ingredients to the dry ingredients, stirring until just combined.

3. Bake the Cupcakes:

   - Divide the batter evenly among the cupcake liners, filling each about 2/3 full.

   - Bake for 18-20 minutes, or until a toothpick inserted into the center of a cupcake comes out clean.

   - Remove from the oven and allow the cupcakes to cool completely on a wire rack before frosting.

4. Make the Frosting:

   - In a medium bowl, beat the softened cream cheese and butter together until smooth and creamy.

   - Gradually add the powdered sugar and beat until light and fluffy.

   - Mix in the vanilla extract.

5. Decorate the Cupcakes:

   - Once the cupcakes are completely cool, frost each one with the cream cheese frosting.

   - Place two mini pretzels at the top of each cupcake to resemble Rudolph's antlers.

   - Add candy eyes just below the pretzels.

   - Press a red candy into the center of each cupcake for Rudolph's nose.

6. Serve:

   - Your "Rudolph's Red Velvet Cupcakes" are ready to serve! Arrange them on a festive platter and enjoy.

These "Rudolph's Red Velvet Cupcakes" are a festive and adorable holiday dessert, perfect for Christmas parties or as a fun baking activity with kids!

35. Peppermint Bark Pretzels

Chocolate-covered pretzels with crushed peppermint candies.

Ingredients:

- 2 cups mini pretzels (or pretzel rods)

- 12 oz white chocolate or white candy melts

- 1/2 teaspoon peppermint extract (optional)

- 1/2 cup crushed candy canes or peppermint candies

- 6 oz dark chocolate or semi-sweet chocolate chips

Instructions:

1. **Melt the White Chocolate:**

   - In a microwave-safe bowl, melt the white chocolate or white candy melts in 20-second intervals, stirring between each, until fully melted and smooth.

   - If using peppermint extract, stir it into the melted white chocolate.

2. **Dip the Pretzels:**

   - Line a baking sheet with parchment paper or wax paper.

   - Dip each mini pretzel into the melted white chocolate, covering about half of the pretzel.

   - Gently tap off any excess chocolate and place the dipped pretzels onto the prepared baking sheet.

3. **Sprinkle with Crushed Candy Canes:**

   - While the white chocolate is still wet, sprinkle the crushed candy canes or peppermint candies over the dipped portion of each pretzel.

4. **Melt the Dark Chocolate:**

   - In another microwave-safe bowl, melt the dark chocolate or chocolate chips in 20-second intervals, stirring between each, until fully melted and smooth.

5. **Drizzle the Dark Chocolate:**

   - Using a spoon or piping bag, drizzle the melted dark chocolate over the white chocolate-coated pretzels for a decorative effect.

6. **Set the Pretzels:**

   - Allow the pretzels to cool and the chocolate to harden completely at room temperature, or place them in the refrigerator for 10-15 minutes to speed up the process.

7. **Serve or Package:**

- Once the chocolate is set, the "Peppermint Bark Pretzels" are ready to enjoy! Serve them on a holiday platter or package them in festive treat bags for gifting.

These "Peppermint Bark Pretzels" are the perfect sweet and salty holiday treat, combining the classic flavors of peppermint and chocolate with the crunch of pretzels. They're great for snacking, gifting, or adding to your holiday dessert spread!

36. Christmas Ornament Popcorn Balls

Popcorn balls shaped like holiday ornaments.

Ingredients:

- 1/2 cup popcorn kernels (or 12 cups pre-popped popcorn)

- 1 cup granulated sugar

- 1/2 cup light corn syrup

- 1/2 cup unsalted butter

- 1/2 teaspoon salt

- 1 teaspoon vanilla extract

- Food coloring (red, green, or your choice)

- Assorted candy (M&Ms, sprinkles, or other colorful candies for decoration)

- Cooking spray or oil (for hands)

Instructions:

1. Pop the Popcorn:

   - If using popcorn kernels, pop them according to your preferred method (stovetop, air popper, etc.) and place the popped popcorn in a large bowl, removing any unpopped kernels.

2. Prepare the Syrup:

   - In a medium saucepan, combine the granulated sugar, corn syrup, butter, and salt. Cook over medium heat, stirring until the mixture comes to a boil.

   - Once boiling, stop stirring and let it boil for 2-3 minutes without stirring until it reaches a soft-ball stage (approximately 240°F or 115°C on a candy thermometer).

3. Add Flavor and Color:

   - Remove the saucepan from the heat and stir in the vanilla extract. If desired, add a few drops of food coloring to the syrup and mix until you achieve your desired color.

4. **Combine Popcorn and Syrup:**

   - Pour the syrup over the popped popcorn and quickly stir to coat the popcorn evenly. Be careful, as the syrup will be very hot.

5. **Shape the Popcorn Balls:**

   - Let the mixture cool for a few minutes until it is manageable but still warm. Lightly grease your hands with cooking spray or oil.

   - Grab small handfuls of the popcorn mixture and shape them into balls, about the size of a small orange. If desired, press assorted candy into the balls for decoration.

6. **Cool and Set:**

   - Place the popcorn balls on a parchment-lined baking sheet or wax paper to cool completely and harden.

7. **Serve or Package:**

   - Once cooled, the "Christmas Ornament Popcorn Balls" are ready to serve! You can place them in decorative bags or boxes for gifting or add a festive ribbon for decoration.

These "Christmas Ornament Popcorn Balls" are a delightful and festive treat, perfect for holiday gatherings, parties, or as a fun activity to make with kids!

37. Santa's Reindeer Carrot Smoothie

A nutritious carrot smoothie to sustain Santa's reindeer.

Ingredients:

- 1 cup fresh baby carrots (or 2 medium carrots, peeled and chopped)

- 1 banana, frozen

- 1 cup orange juice (or almond milk for a creamier option)

- 1/2 cup plain or vanilla yogurt (optional for creaminess)

- 1 tablespoon honey or maple syrup (optional, adjust to taste)

- 1/2 teaspoon ground cinnamon (optional)

- 1/2 teaspoon vanilla extract

- Ice cubes (optional, for a thicker smoothie)

Instructions:

1. Prepare the Carrots:

  - If using whole carrots, peel and chop them into smaller pieces to make blending easier.

2. Blend the Ingredients:

  - In a blender, combine the baby carrots, frozen banana, orange juice (or almond milk), yogurt (if using), honey or maple syrup, cinnamon (if using), and vanilla extract.

  - Blend on high speed until the mixture is smooth and creamy. If the smoothie is too thick, add more juice or milk to reach your desired consistency.

3. Adjust Sweetness:

  - Taste the smoothie and adjust sweetness if necessary by adding more honey or syrup, then blend again briefly to combine.

4. Serve:

  - Pour the smoothie into glasses. If desired, you can garnish with a sprinkle of cinnamon on top or a few carrot sticks for decoration.

5. Enjoy:

  - Serve immediately for the best flavor and freshness. This smoothie can be enjoyed as a healthy breakfast, snack, or festive treat for the holidays!

38. *Sugar Plum Fairy Fruit Salad*

A stunning combination of vibrant fruits for a delectable delight.

Ingredients:

- 6 ripe sugar plums (pitted and sliced)

- 1 cup strawberries (hulled and halved)

- 1 cup blueberries

- 1 cup green grapes (halved)

- 1 cup pineapple chunks (fresh or canned)

- 1/2 cup pomegranate seeds

- 2 tablespoons fresh mint leaves (finely chopped)

- 1 tablespoon honey (optional)

- 1 tablespoon lime juice

- Zest of 1 lime

Instructions:

1. Prepare the fruit:

  - Pit and slice the sugar plums.

  - Hull and halve the strawberries.

  - Halve the grapes.

  - Drain the pineapple chunks if using canned.

2. Mix the salad:

  - In a large bowl, combine the sugar plums, strawberries, blueberries, grapes, pineapple chunks, and pomegranate seeds.

3. Prepare the dressing:

  - In a small bowl, whisk together the lime juice, honey (optional), and lime zest.

4. Toss the salad:

- Pour the dressing over the fruit and gently toss to combine.

5. Garnish:

- Sprinkle the chopped mint leaves over the top and give the salad a final light toss.

6. Chill and serve:

- Refrigerate the salad for 20-30 minutes to let the flavors meld.

- Serve chilled, and enjoy!

39. Elf-Sized Gingerbread Houses

Small gingerbread houses ideal for elves to enjoy.

Ingredients:

Gingerbread Dough:

- 2 3/4 cups all-purpose flour

- 1 tablespoon ground ginger

- 1 tablespoon ground cinnamon

- 1/2 teaspoon ground nutmeg

- 1/2 teaspoon ground cloves

- 1/2 teaspoon baking soda

- 1/2 teaspoon salt

- 1/2 cup unsalted butter (room temperature)

- 1/2 cup packed brown sugar

- 1/2 cup molasses

- 1 large egg

- 1 teaspoon vanilla extract

Royal Icing (for glue and decorating):

- 2 large egg whites (or 4 tablespoons meringue powder and 1/2 cup water)

- 3 cups powdered sugar

- 1/2 teaspoon cream of tartar

- Food coloring (optional)

- Sprinkles, candy, and other small decorations

Tools:

- Gingerbread house templates (scaled down for elf-size)

- Piping bags with small tips

- Rolling pin

- Baking sheets

- Parchment paper

Instructions:

Step 1: Make the Gingerbread Dough

1. Mix dry ingredients:

   - In a medium bowl, whisk together flour, ginger, cinnamon, nutmeg, cloves, baking soda, and salt.

2. Cream butter and sugar:

   - In a large bowl, cream together the butter and brown sugar until light and fluffy.

3. Add wet ingredients:

   - Beat in the molasses, egg, and vanilla extract until well combined.

4. Combine:

   - Gradually add the dry ingredients to the wet mixture, mixing until a stiff dough forms. Divide the dough in half, flatten into disks, and wrap in plastic wrap. Refrigerate for at least 1 hour.

Step 2: Roll Out and Bake

1. Preheat

   - Oven to 350°F (175°C). Line baking sheets with parchment paper.

2. Roll out dough:

   - On a lightly floured surface, roll out the chilled dough to about 1/8 inch thickness.

3. Cut the house pieces:

   - Use the gingerbread house templates to cut out the walls, roof, and other pieces. You'll need 4 walls and 2 roof pieces per house.

4. Bake:

   - Place the pieces on the prepared baking sheets and bake for 8-10 minutes, until the edges are firm. Let them cool completely on the baking sheets.

Step 3: Make the Royal Icing (Glue)

1. Mix icing:

   - In a large bowl, beat the egg whites (or meringue powder mixture) and cream of tartar until frothy. Gradually add powdered sugar, beating until stiff peaks form.

2. Prepare piping bags:

  - Fill piping bags with the icing. If using food coloring, divide the icing into portions and color as desired.

Step 4: Assemble and Decorate

1. Assemble the house:

  - Use the royal icing to "glue" the gingerbread pieces together. Start by attaching the walls and holding them in place for a few minutes until set. Then add the roof. Let the structure sit for at least 15 minutes to firm up.

2. Decorate:

  - Use more royal icing to decorate the house with sprinkles, candy, or other decorations. Pipe windows, doors, and any other details you like.

3. Let the houses set:

  - Allow the icing to fully harden before handling or displaying your elf-sized gingerbread houses.

40. Jolly Gingerbread Cupcakes

Soft gingerbread cupcakes with festive icing.

Ingredients:

For the Cupcakes:

- 1 1/2 cups all-purpose flour

- 1 teaspoon baking soda

- 1/2 teaspoon baking powder

- 1 1/2 teaspoons ground ginger

- 1 teaspoon ground cinnamon

- 1/4 teaspoon ground nutmeg

- 1/4 teaspoon ground cloves

- 1/4 teaspoon salt

- 1/2 cup unsalted butter (room temperature)

- 1/2 cup granulated sugar

- 1/2 cup molasses

- 1 large egg (room temperature)

- 1 teaspoon vanilla extract

- 1/2 cup buttermilk (room temperature)

For the Cream Cheese Frosting:

- 8 oz cream cheese (softened)

- 1/4 cup unsalted butter (softened)

- 2 1/2 cups powdered sugar

- 1 teaspoon vanilla extract

- 1/2 teaspoon ground cinnamon (optional)

Decorations:

- Gingerbread cookie sprinkles or mini gingerbread cookies

- Festive holiday sprinkles (optional)

Instructions:

Step 1: Make the Cupcakes

1. Preheat oven:

   - Preheat the oven to 350°F (175°C). Line a 12-cup muffin pan with cupcake liners.

2. Mix dry ingredients:

   - In a medium bowl, whisk together the flour, baking soda, baking powder, ginger, cinnamon, nutmeg, cloves, and salt.

3. Cream butter and sugar:

   - In a large bowl, beat the butter and granulated sugar together until light and fluffy, about 2-3 minutes.

4. Add molasses, egg, and vanilla:

   - Beat in the molasses, egg, and vanilla extract until smooth.

5. Alternate dry ingredients and buttermilk:

   - Gradually add the dry ingredients to the wet mixture in three parts, alternating with the buttermilk. Start and end with the dry ingredients, mixing until just combined.

6. Fill cupcake liners:

   - Spoon the batter into the prepared cupcake liners, filling each about 2/3 full.

7. Bake:

   - Bake for 18-20 minutes, or until a toothpick inserted into the center comes out clean. Let the cupcakes cool in the pan for 5 minutes, then transfer to a wire rack to cool completely.

Step 2: Make the Cream Cheese Frosting

1. Beat cream cheese and butter:

  - In a large bowl, beat the softened cream cheese and butter together until smooth and creamy.

2. Add powdered sugar and vanilla:

  - Gradually add the powdered sugar, beating until fluffy and well combined. Add the vanilla extract and ground cinnamon (if using) and mix well.

Step 3: Frost and Decorate

1. Frost the cupcakes:

  - Once the cupcakes are completely cooled, frost them with the cream cheese frosting using a piping bag or spatula.

2. Decorate:

  - Top with mini gingerbread cookies or festive holiday sprinkles to give them a jolly holiday look.

3. Serve and enjoy:

  - Serve these gingerbread cupcakes at holiday gatherings or enjoy with a warm cup of cocoa!

41. Peppermint Patty Snowballs

Chocolate and peppermint snowball-shaped sweets.

Ingredients:

For the Snowballs:

- 1 cup unsalted butter (softened)

- 1/2 cup powdered sugar

- 1 teaspoon vanilla extract

- 1/4 teaspoon peppermint extract

- 2 1/4 cups all-purpose flour

- 1/4 teaspoon salt

- 1/2 cup mini chocolate chips

- 1/2 cup crushed peppermint candies (or candy canes)

For Rolling:

- 1 cup powdered sugar

- 1/4 cup crushed peppermint candies (for garnish)

Instructions:

Step 1: Prepare the Dough

1. Cream butter and sugar:

   - In a large mixing bowl, cream together the softened butter and 1/2 cup powdered sugar until light and fluffy.

2. Add extracts:

   - Mix in the vanilla extract and peppermint extract.

3. Mix dry ingredients:

   - In a separate bowl, whisk together the flour and salt.

4. Combine the mixtures:

   - Gradually add the dry ingredients to the butter mixture, stirring until just combined.

5. Add chocolate and peppermint:

   - Gently fold in the mini chocolate chips and crushed peppermint candies.

6. Chill the dough:

   - Cover the dough and refrigerate for about 30 minutes to make it easier to handle.

Step 2: Form and Bake

1. Preheat the oven:

   - Preheat your oven to 350°F (175°C). Line a baking sheet with parchment paper.

2. Shape the snowballs:

   - Roll the chilled dough into 1-inch balls and place them on the prepared baking sheet, spacing them about 1 inch apart.

3. Bake:

   - Bake for 12-15 minutes, or until the bottoms are lightly golden. The tops should remain pale. Remove from the oven and let them cool for 5 minutes.

Step 3: Roll in Powdered Sugar

1. Prepare rolling sugar:

   - In a shallow bowl, combine the remaining 1 cup of powdered sugar with the additional crushed peppermint candies.

2. Roll the snowballs:

   - While the cookies are still warm, roll them in the powdered sugar mixture, making sure they are well coated.

3. Cool and roll again:

   - Let the cookies cool completely, then roll them in the powdered sugar one more time for an extra snowy look.

Step 4: Serve and Enjoy

- Arrange the Peppermint Patty Snowballs on a festive plate and serve! They are perfect for holiday cookie exchanges, winter parties, or as a sweet treat with a cup of hot cocoa.

42. Snowman Cheese Ball

A cheesy snowman snack on crackers.

Ingredients:

 For the Cheese Ball:

- 16 oz cream cheese (softened)

- 2 cups shredded sharp cheddar cheese

- 1 tablespoon ranch seasoning mix

- 1 teaspoon garlic powder

- 1/2 teaspoon onion powder

- 1/4 teaspoon black pepper

- 1/4 cup chopped chives or green onions (optional)

For the Snowman Decoration:

- 1/2 cup finely shredded mozzarella cheese (for coating)

- 2 whole black olives (for eyes)

- 1 small carrot (for nose)

- 3-4 pretzel sticks (for arms)

- Black peppercorns or small black olives (for buttons and mouth)

- Fresh parsley or rosemary sprigs (for scarf or hat, optional)

Instructions:

Step 1: Make the Cheese Ball Mixture

1. Mix the cheese:

  - In a large bowl, combine the softened cream cheese, shredded cheddar cheese, ranch seasoning, garlic powder, onion powder, black pepper, and chives (if using). Mix until all ingredients are fully combined.

2. Shape the snowman:

  - Divide the mixture into three portions: one large for the base, one medium for the body, and one small for the head.

  - Shape each portion into a ball.

3. Chill the cheese balls:

  - Wrap each cheese ball in plastic wrap and refrigerate for at least 1 hour to firm up.

Step 2: Assemble the Snowman

1. Coat the cheese balls:

- Roll each cheese ball in finely shredded mozzarella cheese to give it a snow-like appearance.

2. Stack the snowman:

- Place the largest ball on a serving platter as the base. Stack the medium-sized ball on top for the body, and finally, the smallest ball on top as the head.

Step 3: Decorate the Snowman

1. Add the eyes and nose:

- Use two black olives for the eyes and a small piece of carrot for the snowman's nose.

2. Make the mouth and buttons:

- Place peppercorns or small olive pieces in a smile shape for the mouth. Add additional peppercorns or olive pieces down the body for buttons.

3. Add arms and scarf (optional):

- Insert pretzel sticks on each side of the snowman for arms. Use sprigs of fresh parsley or rosemary to create a scarf or a festive hat if desired.

Step 4: Serve

- Serve with: Crackers, sliced veggies, or breadsticks for dipping.

43. Grinch Green Smoothie

A refreshing green smoothie that is both nutritious and enjoyable.

Ingredients:

- 1 ripe banana

- 1/2 cup fresh spinach (packed)

- 1/2 cup frozen pineapple chunks

- 1/2 cup frozen mango chunks

- 1/2 cup unsweetened almond milk (or any milk of your choice)

- 1/4 cup plain Greek yogurt (optional for creaminess)

- 1 tablespoon honey or maple syrup (optional for sweetness)

- 1/2 teaspoon vanilla extract

- 1 tablespoon chia seeds (optional for extra nutrition)

For Decoration (Optional):

- Red heart-shaped sprinkle (for the "Grinch" theme)

Instructions:

Step 1: Blend the Ingredients

1. Add ingredients to blender:

   - Place the banana, spinach, frozen pineapple, frozen mango, almond milk, Greek yogurt (if using), honey (if using), vanilla extract, and chia seeds in a blender.

2. Blend until smooth:

   - Blend on high until all the ingredients are smooth and well combined. If the smoothie is too thick, add a little more almond milk until you reach your desired consistency.

Step 2: Serve

1. Pour into glasses:

   - Pour the smoothie into a tall glass or jar.

2. Add a Grinchy touch:

   - For a fun touch, place a red heart-shaped sprinkle on the side of the glass or on top of the smoothie to mimic the Grinch's growing heart!

Step 3: Enjoy

- Sip on this healthy, vibrant green smoothie for a delicious and nutritious treat that's perfect for breakfast or a holiday snack.

44. Santa's Stovetop S'mores

Traditional s'mores made with marshmallows on the burner.

Ingredients:

- 12 graham cracker squares

- 6 large marshmallows

- 6 squares of milk chocolate (or your favorite chocolate)

- 1 tablespoon butter (optional, for toasting marshmallows)

- Red and green sprinkles (optional, for a festive touch)

- Mini candy canes or holiday-themed chocolates (optional, for garnish)

Instructions:

Step 1: Prepare the Ingredients

1. Break the graham crackers and chocolate:

- Break each graham cracker square in half, so you have 12 smaller squares.

- Prepare 6 chocolate squares, one for each s'more.

2. Prepare the marshmallows:

- If you want extra flavor, dip the marshmallows in butter for a golden, toasty finish.

Step 2: Toast the Marshmallows

1. Stovetop method:

- Place a marshmallow on a fork or skewer.

- Carefully toast the marshmallow over a low flame on the stovetop or use a kitchen torch until it becomes golden brown and gooey. Rotate the marshmallow to ensure it toasts evenly.

Step 3: Assemble the S'mores

1. Layer the s'more:

- Place one square of chocolate on top of a graham cracker. Place the toasted marshmallow on top of the chocolate, and cover with another graham cracker square to create a sandwich.

2. Press gently:

- Gently press the graham crackers together to melt the chocolate slightly with the warmth of the marshmallow.

Step 4: Add Festive Touches

1. Sprinkle decorations:

- If desired, roll the edges of the gooey marshmallow in red and green sprinkles for a festive look.

2. Garnish (optional):

   - Serve with mini candy canes or holiday-themed chocolates on the side for a festive presentation.

Step 5: Serve and Enjoy

- Serve immediately while warm and gooey. These stovetop s'mores are perfect for a holiday movie night or a fun snack to share with family and friends.

45. Reindeer Trail Mix

A festive Christmas snack combination ideal for both youngsters and reindeer.

Ingredients:

- 1 cup pretzel twists or sticks

- 1 cup mini marshmallows

- 1 cup chocolate-covered peanuts or regular peanuts

- 1 cup red and green candy-coated chocolates (like M&Ms)

- 1 cup dried cranberries or raisins

- 1/2 cup yogurt-covered raisins (optional)

- 1/2 cup mini peanut butter cups or chocolate chips

- 1/2 cup holiday-themed sprinkles (optional for a festive touch)

Instructions:

Step 1: Prepare the Ingredients

1. Gather and measure:

   - Measure out all the ingredients and place them in separate bowls for easy mixing.

Step 2: Mix the Ingredients

1. Combine in a large bowl:

   - In a large mixing bowl, combine the pretzels, mini marshmallows, peanuts, candy-coated chocolates, dried cranberries, yogurt-covered raisins, mini peanut butter cups, and sprinkles (if using).

2. Toss gently:

   - Gently toss the ingredients together until they are evenly mixed.

Step 3: Serve

1. Serve in a festive bowl or bag:

   - Pour the Reindeer Trail Mix into a holiday-themed bowl or portion it into small treat bags for individual servings.

2. Optional:

   - Add a festive ribbon or tag to the bags to give them as holiday gifts or party favors.

Step 4: Enjoy

- Enjoy the mix as a quick snack, holiday treat, or even a fun party favor for kids and adults alike.

46. Holiday Cinnamon Roll Christmas Trees

Cinnamon buns made into Christmas trees.

Ingredients:

For the Cinnamon Roll Dough:

- 2 1/4 teaspoons active dry yeast (1 packet)

- 1 cup warm milk (110°F/43°C)

- 1/4 cup granulated sugar

- 1/4 cup unsalted butter (melted)

- 1 large egg

- 3 1/2 cups all-purpose flour

- 1/2 teaspoon salt

For the Cinnamon Filling:

- 1/4 cup unsalted butter (softened)

- 1/2 cup brown sugar (packed)

- 2 tablespoons ground cinnamon

For the Icing:

- 1 cup powdered sugar

- 2 tablespoons milk (add more as needed for consistency)

- 1/2 teaspoon vanilla extract

- Green food coloring

For Decoration:

- Red and green sprinkles

- Mini candy stars or yellow sprinkles (for tree toppers)

- Pretzel sticks (for tree trunks)

Instructions:

Step 1: Make the Dough

1. Activate the yeast:

  - In a small bowl, dissolve the yeast in the warm milk. Let it sit for 5-10 minutes until foamy.

2. Mix wet ingredients:

  - In a large bowl, combine the melted butter, sugar, egg, and activated yeast mixture.

3. Add dry ingredients:

   - Gradually add the flour and salt, mixing until a soft dough forms. Knead the dough on a floured surface for 5-7 minutes until smooth and elastic.

4. Let the dough rise:

   - Place the dough in a greased bowl, cover with a clean kitchen towel, and let it rise in a warm place for about 1 hour, or until it doubles in size.

Step 2: Make the Cinnamon Filling

1. Mix the filling:

   - In a small bowl, mix together the softened butter, brown sugar, and cinnamon to create the cinnamon filling.

Step 3: Roll and Shape the Dough

1. Roll out the dough:

   - Once the dough has risen, punch it down and roll it out on a floured surface into a rectangle about 1/4-inch thick.

2. Spread the filling:

   - Evenly spread the cinnamon filling over the dough.

3. Cut and shape into trees:

   - Roll the dough into a tight log from the longer side. Cut the log into 12 even slices. To create the Christmas tree shape, gently squeeze one side of each slice to form a triangle (tree shape).

4. Add the tree trunks:

   - Insert a small pretzel stick into the bottom of each cinnamon roll to form the tree trunk.

Step 4: Bake the Cinnamon Rolls

1. Preheat the oven:

   - Preheat your oven to 350°F (175°C).

2. Bake:

   - Place the cinnamon rolls on a greased or parchment-lined baking sheet and bake for 15-18 minutes, or until golden brown.

Step 5: Decorate the Christmas Trees

1. Make the icing:

   - In a small bowl, whisk together the powdered sugar, milk, and vanilla extract. Add green food coloring to the icing to create a tree-like color.

2. Drizzle or pipe the icing:

   - Once the cinnamon rolls are slightly cooled, drizzle or pipe the green icing over the rolls to resemble Christmas tree garlands.

3. Add decorations:

   - Decorate the trees with red and green sprinkles to look like ornaments, and place a mini candy star or yellow sprinkle on top of each tree.

Step 6: Serve and Enjoy

- Serve these Holiday Cinnamon Roll Christmas Trees warm with your favorite holiday drinks, like hot cocoa or spiced cider!

47. Red and Green Cookie Pops

Cookie pops topped with festive red and green frosting.

Ingredients:

For the Cookies:

- 2 3/4 cups all-purpose flour

- 1 teaspoon baking powder

- 1/2 teaspoon salt

- 1 cup unsalted butter (softened)

- 1 1/2 cups granulated sugar

- 1 large egg

- 1 teaspoon vanilla extract

- Red and green food coloring

For the Decorations:

- Lollipop sticks or popsicle sticks

- Red and green sprinkles

- 1 cup white chocolate chips or candy melts (optional, for dipping)

- Holiday-themed ribbons (optional, for wrapping)

Instructions:

Step 1: Make the Cookie Dough

1. Mix dry ingredients:

   - In a medium bowl, whisk together the flour, baking powder, and salt.

2. Cream butter and sugar:

   - In a large bowl, beat the softened butter and granulated sugar together until light and fluffy, about 2-3 minutes.

3. Add egg and vanilla:

   - Beat in the egg and vanilla extract until fully combined.

4. Combine the dry and wet ingredients:

   - Gradually add the dry ingredients to the butter mixture, mixing until a soft dough forms.

Step 2: Divide and Color the Dough

1. Divide the dough:

- Split the cookie dough into two equal portions.

2. Add color:

- In one portion, mix in red food coloring until you achieve the desired shade of red. In the other portion, mix in green food coloring. Knead the dough until the color is evenly distributed.

Step 3: Shape the Cookies

1. Preheat the oven:

- Preheat your oven to 350°F (175°C). Line a baking sheet with parchment paper.

2. Form the cookie pops:

- Roll small balls of dough (about 1 tablespoon each) in both red and green colors. Press each ball onto the end of a lollipop stick or popsicle stick and flatten slightly.

3. Add sprinkles:

- Decorate the cookies with red and green sprinkles before baking, or leave them plain if you want to dip them in chocolate later.

Step 4: Bake the Cookies

1. Bake:

- Place the cookie pops on the prepared baking sheet and bake for 8-10 minutes, or until the edges are lightly golden. Let them cool on the baking sheet for a few minutes before transferring them to a wire rack to cool completely.

Step 5: Optional Chocolate Dipping

1. Melt the chocolate:

- If you want to dip the cookie pops in chocolate, melt the white chocolate chips or candy melts in a microwave-safe bowl, stirring every 20 seconds until smooth.

2. Dip the cookies:

- Dip the tops of the cooled cookie pops into the melted chocolate, then sprinkle with additional red and green sprinkles for a festive look.

Step 6: Serve and Wrap

1. Let the chocolate set:

- Allow the dipped cookie pops to sit until the chocolate hardens, or place them in the fridge for a few minutes to speed up the process.

2. Optional wrapping:

- If giving as gifts, wrap each cookie pop in a small plastic bag and tie with holiday-themed ribbon.

Step 7: Enjoy!

- These Red and Green Cookie Pops are perfect for holiday parties, gift exchanges, or as a fun activity with kids. Serve them on a festive plate or wrap them up as a treat for friends and family.

The pops are a festive, portable treat that adds holiday cheer to any gathering!

48. Santa's Beard Banana Bites

To simulate Santa's beard, cut banana slices and top with coconut.

Ingredients:

- 2 ripe bananas

- 1/2 cup shredded coconut (for Santa's beard)

- 1/4 cup vanilla yogurt (for dipping)

- 1/4 cup mini chocolate chips (for eyes)

- 1/4 cup red candy-coated chocolates or red M&Ms (for the nose)

- 6 pretzel sticks (for the hat or optional decorations)

- 12 small toothpicks or decorative food picks

Instructions:

Step 1: Prepare the Ingredients

1. Peel and slice bananas:

  - Peel the bananas and slice them into 1-inch thick rounds.

2. Set up dipping and coating:

  - Place the shredded coconut on a plate and the vanilla yogurt in a small bowl for easy dipping.

Step 2: Assemble the Banana Bites

1. Dip in yogurt:

  - Using a toothpick or food pick, dip each banana slice halfway into the vanilla yogurt to coat the bottom half of the banana.

2. Coat with coconut:

  - Immediately roll the yogurt-covered portion of the banana in shredded coconut to create Santa's beard.

3. Add the eyes and nose:

  - Place two mini chocolate chips on the top portion of the banana slice for Santa's eyes.

  - Press a red candy-coated chocolate (or M&M) below the eyes to make Santa's nose.

4. Optional Hat Decoration:

  - Break a pretzel stick in half and insert it into the top of the banana slice to create a simple "hat" for Santa.

1. Chill (optional):

  - For a colder treat, place the Santa's Beard Banana Bites in the fridge for about 15 minutes to let the yogurt firm up.

2. Serve immediately:

  - Arrange the banana bites on a festive serving plate, and enjoy this quick and healthy holiday snack.

These Santa's Beard Banana Bites are a fun and festive snack, perfect for kids and holiday gatherings! They're quick to make, healthy, and add a playful twist to your holiday treats.

49. Gingerbread Pancakes with Whipped Cream

Fluffy gingerbread pancakes with whipped cream.

Ingredients:

For the Gingerbread Pancakes:

- 1 1/2 cups all-purpose flour

- 2 teaspoons baking powder

- 1/4 teaspoon baking soda

- 1/4 teaspoon salt

- 1 teaspoon ground ginger

- 1 teaspoon ground cinnamon

- 1/4 teaspoon ground nutmeg

- 1/4 teaspoon ground cloves

- 2 tablespoons brown sugar (packed)

- 1 egg

- 1 cup milk (or buttermilk)

- 2 tablespoons molasses

- 2 tablespoons unsalted butter (melted)

- 1 teaspoon vanilla extract

For the Whipped Cream:

- 1 cup heavy whipping cream

- 2 tablespoons powdered sugar

- 1/2 teaspoon vanilla extract

Optional Toppings:

- Maple syrup

- Ground cinnamon (for dusting)

- Crushed gingerbread cookies (for garnish)

- Fresh berries (optional)

Instructions:

Step 1: Make the Pancake Batter

1. Mix dry ingredients:

  - In a large bowl, whisk together the flour, baking powder, baking soda, salt, ginger, cinnamon, nutmeg, cloves, and brown sugar.

2. Whisk wet ingredients:

   - In a separate bowl, whisk the egg, milk, molasses, melted butter, and vanilla extract until well combined.

3. Combine wet and dry ingredients:

   - Gradually add the wet ingredients to the dry ingredients, mixing just until combined. Be careful not to overmix; a few lumps are fine.

Step 2: Cook the Pancakes

1. Preheat the skillet:

   - Heat a non-stick skillet or griddle over medium heat and lightly grease with butter or oil.

2. Cook pancakes:

   - Pour 1/4 cup of batter onto the skillet for each pancake. Cook until bubbles form on the surface and the edges start to set, about 2-3 minutes. Flip and cook for another 1-2 minutes, until golden brown and cooked through.

3. Keep warm:

   - Transfer cooked pancakes to a plate and cover loosely with foil to keep warm while you cook the remaining batter.

Step 3: Make the Whipped Cream

1. Whip the cream:

   - In a chilled bowl, beat the heavy cream, powdered sugar, and vanilla extract with a hand mixer or whisk until soft peaks form.

2. Set aside:

   - Refrigerate the whipped cream until ready to serve.

Step 4: Serve the Pancakes

1. Stack the pancakes:

   - Stack the gingerbread pancakes on a plate.

2. Top with whipped cream:

   - Spoon a generous dollop of homemade whipped cream on top of the pancakes.

3. Add optional toppings:

   - Drizzle with maple syrup, dust with a little extra cinnamon, and garnish with crushed gingerbread cookies or fresh berries for a festive touch.

Step 5: Enjoy!

- Serve these Gingerbread Pancakes with Whipped Cream warm for a delicious and festive breakfast perfect for the holiday season.

These pancakes are packed with gingerbread spices, making them the perfect cozy breakfast treat!

50. Christmas Tree Brownie Bites

Brownie bites molded and decorated as Christmas trees.

Ingredients:

For the Brownies:

- 1/2 cup unsalted butter (melted)

- 1 cup granulated sugar

- 2 large eggs

- 1 teaspoon vanilla extract

- 1/3 cup cocoa powder

- 1/2 cup all-purpose flour

- 1/4 teaspoon baking powder

- 1/4 teaspoon salt

For Decoration:

- 1/2 cup green frosting (store-bought or homemade)

- Mini candy stars or yellow sprinkles (for the tree toppers)

- Red and green sprinkles

- Pretzel sticks (for tree trunks)

- Powdered sugar (optional for dusting)

Instructions:

Step 1: Make the Brownies

1. Preheat the oven:

   - Preheat your oven to 350°F (175°C). Grease a square 8x8-inch baking pan or line it with parchment paper.

2. Mix wet ingredients:

   - In a medium bowl, whisk together the melted butter, sugar, eggs, and vanilla extract until smooth and well combined.

3. Mix dry ingredients:

   - In a separate bowl, sift together the cocoa powder, flour, baking powder, and salt.

4. Combine wet and dry ingredients:

   - Gradually add the dry ingredients to the wet mixture, stirring just until combined.

5. Bake:

   - Pour the brownie batter into the prepared pan and smooth the top. Bake for 20-25 minutes or until a toothpick inserted into the center comes out with moist crumbs.

6. Cool:

   - Let the brownies cool completely in the pan before cutting.

Step 2: Cut and Shape the Brownies

1. Cut into triangles:

   - Once the brownies are cooled, cut them into triangles to resemble Christmas tree shapes. You can make small triangles by cutting the brownies into strips, then cutting each strip into alternating triangles.

2. Insert pretzel sticks:

   - Gently insert a pretzel stick into the base of each brownie triangle to create the "tree trunk."

Step 3: Decorate the Brownie Trees

1. Frosting:

   - Spoon the green frosting into a piping bag or zip-top bag with a small corner cut off. Pipe the frosting onto each brownie in a zig-zag pattern to resemble garland on the trees.

2. Add sprinkles:

   - Decorate the frosted brownies with red and green sprinkles to mimic Christmas ornaments.

3. Add a star:

   - Place a mini candy star or yellow sprinkle at the top of each tree for the tree topper.

Step 4: Serve and Enjoy

1. Optional dusting:

- Lightly dust the trees with powdered sugar for a snowy effect (optional).

2. Serve:

  - Arrange the Christmas Tree Brownie Bites on a festive platter and enjoy!

These cute and festive brownie bites are perfect for holiday parties, as a gift, or as a fun treat to make with kids!

Thank you for reading this book. I hope you enjoy reading about all of these big trucks.

Please leave a review; it helps other people know they can enjoy this book.